ALISTAIR MACLEAN

Alistair MacLean, the son of a Scots minister, was born in 1922 and brought up in the Scottish Highlands. In 1941 at the age of eighteen he joined the Royal Navy; two-and-a-half years spent aboard a cruiser was later to give him the background for HMS *Ulysses*, his first novel, the outstanding documentary novel on the war at sea. After the war, he gained an English Honours degree at Glasgow University, and became a school master. In 1983 he was awarded a D.Litt from the same university.

He is now recognized as one of the outstanding popular writers of the 20th century. By the early 1970s he was one of the top 10 bestselling authors in the world, and the biggest-selling Briton. He wrote twenty-nine worldwide best-sellers that have sold more than 30 million copies, and many of which have been filmed, including *The Guns of Navarone*, *Where Eagles Dare*, *Fear is the Key* and *Ice Station Zebra*. Alistair MacLean died in 1987 at his home in Switzerland.

By Alistair MacLean

ALISTAIR MACLEAN

The Lonely Sea

Collected Short Stories

HARPER

Harper
An imprint of HarperCollins*Publishers*
77–85 Fulham Palace Road,
Hammersmith, London W6 8JB

www.harpercollins.co.uk

This paperback edition 2009
1

First published in Great Britain by
William Collins Sons & Co. Ltd 1985
then in paperback by Fontana 1986

*City of Benares, The Arandora Star, Rawalpindi,
The Meknes, The Jervis Bay* and *Lancastria*
published by the *Sunday Express* 1960.

*Rewards and Responsibilites of Success,
The Black Storm* and *The Good Samaritan* published by
the Glasgow Herald 1982, 1995 and 1996.

A catalogue record for this book is
available from the British Library

ISBN 978-0-00-789229-7

Typeset in Meridien by Thomson Digital, India

Printed and bound in Great Britain by
Clays Ltd, St Ives plc

Mixed Sources
Product group from well-managed
forests and other controlled sources
www.fsc.org Cert no. SW-COC-001806
© 1996 Forest Stewardship Council

FSC is a non-profit international organisation established to promote the
responsible management of the world's forests. Products carrying the FSC
label are independently certified to assure consumers that they come
from forests that are managed to meet the social, economic and
ecological needs of present and future generations.

Find out more about HarperCollins and the environment at
www.harpercollins.co.uk/green

Contents

The Dileas

Three hours gone, Mr MacLean, three hours – and never a word of the lifeboat.

You can imagine just how it was. There were only the four of us there – Eachan, Torry Mor, old Grant, and myself. Talk? Never a word among the lot of us, nor even the heart of a dram – and there on the table, was a new bottle of Talisker, and Eachan not looking for a penny.

We just sat there like a lot of stookies, Seumas Grant with his expressionless face and yon wicked old pipe of his bubbling away, and the rest of us desperately busy with studying the pattern of the wallpaper. Listening to the screech of the wind, we were, and the hail like chuckies battering against the windows of the hotel. Dhia! What a night that was! And the worst of it was, we couldn't do a thing but wait. My, but we were a right cheery crowd.

* * *

I think we all gave a wee bit jump when the telephone rang. Eachan hurried away and was back in a moment beaming all over. One look at yon great moonface of his and we felt as if the Pladda Lighthouse had been lifted off our backs.

'Four glasses, gentlemen, and see's over the Talisker. That was the lightkeeper at Creag Dearg. The *Molly Ann* got there in time – just. The puffer's gone, but all the crew were taken off.'

He pushed the glasses over and looked straight at old Grant.

'Well, Seumas, what have you to say now? The *Molly Ann* got there – and Donald Archie and Lachlan away over by Scavaig. Perhaps you would be saying it's a miracle, eh, Seumas?'

There was no love lost between these two, I can tell you. Mind you, most of us were on Eachan's side. He was a hard man, was old Seumas Grant. Well respected, right enough, but no one had any affection for him and, by Jove, he had none for us – none for anyone at all, except for Lachlan and Donald, his sons. For old Seumas, the sun rose to shine on them alone. His motherless sons: for them the croft, for them the boat, for them his every waking thought. But a hard man, Mr Maclean. Aloof and – what's the word? – remote. Kept himself to himself, you might say.

'It's a miracle when anyone is saved on a night like this, Eachan.' Old Grant's voice was slow and deep.

'But without Donald and Lachlan?' Eachan pressed. Torry, I remember shifted in his seat, and I looked away. We didn't care for this too much – it wasn't right.

'Big Neil's weel enough in his own way,' Grant said, kind of quiet. 'But he'll never be the lifeboat coxswain Lachie is – he hasn't got the feel of the sea –'

Just then the hotel door crashed open, nearly lifted off its hinges by the wind. Peter the Post came stumbling in, heaved the door shut and stood there glistening in his oilskins. It only required one look at him to see that something was far wrong.

'The lifeboat, Eachan, the *Molly Ann*!' he jerked out, very quick and urgent. 'Any word of her yet? Hurry, man, hurry!'

Eachan looked at him in surprise.

'Why surely, Peter. We've just heard. She's lying off Creag Dearg and . . .'

'Creag Dearg! Oh Dhia, Dhia, Dhia!' Peter the Post sunk down into a chair and gazed dully into the fire. 'Twenty miles away – twenty miles. And here's Iain Chisholm just in from Tarbert farm – three miles in four minutes on yon big Velocette of his – to say that the Buidhe ferry is out in the middle of the Sound, firing distress rockets. And the *Molly Ann* at Creag Dearg. Mo chreach, mo chreach!' He shook his head slowly from side to side.

'The ferry!' I said stupidly. 'The ferry! Big John must be smashed mad to take her out on a night like this!'

'And every boat in the fishing fleet sheltering up by Loch Torridon like enough,' said Torry bitterly.

There was a long silence, then old Grant was on his feet, still puffing away.

'All except mine, Torry Mor,' he said, buttoning up his oilskins. 'It's God's blessing that Donal' and Lachie went to Scavaig to look over this new drifter.' He stopped and looked slowly around. 'I'm thinking I'll be needing a bit hand.'

We just stared at him, and when Eachan spoke it was like a man in a stound.

'You mean you'll take yon old tub out in this, Seumas?' Eachan was staggered. 'Forty years old if she's a day – and the seas like houses roaring straight down the Sound. Why, you'll be smashed to pieces, man – before you're right clear of the harbour mouth.'

'Lachie would go.' Old Grant stared at the ground. 'He's the coxswain. He would go – and Donal'. I canna be letting my boys down.'

'It's suicide, Mr Grant,' I urged him. 'Like Eachan says, it's almost certain death.'

'There's no almost about it for the poor souls out on that ferry.' He reached for his sou'wester and turned to the door. 'Maybe I'll be managing right enough.'

Eachan flung the counter-flap up with a crash.

'You're a stiff-necked old fool, Seumas Grant,' he shouted angrily, 'and you'll roast in hell for your infernal pride!' He turned back and snatched a couple of bottles of brandy from the shelves. 'Maybe these'll come in handy,' he muttered to himself, then stamped out of the door, growling deep in his throat and scowling something terrible.

Mind you, the *Dileas* – that was old Seumas Grant's boat – was a deal better than Eachan made her out to be. When Campbell of Ardrishaig built a Loch-Fyner, the timbers came out of the heart of the oak. And old Grant had added mild steel frames of his own and installed one of these new-fangled diesels – a 44 hp Gardner, I remember. But even so.

Outside the harbour wall – you couldn't imagine it and you'll never see the like, not even in your blackest nightmares. Bitter cold it was and the whistling sleet just flying lumps of ice that lanced your face open to the bone.

And the Sound itself! Oh Dhia, that Sound! The seas were short and desperate steep, with the speed of racehorses, and the whole Sound a great sheet of driven milk gleaming in yon pitchy blackness. Man, it makes me shudder even now.

For two hours we headed straight up into it, and, Jove, what a wild hammering we took. The

Dileas would totter up on a wave then, like she was falling over a cliff, smash down into the next trough with the crack of a four-inch gun, burying herself right to the gunwales. And at the same time you could hear the fierce clatter of her screw, clawing at the thin air. Why the Dileas never broke her back only God knows – or the ghost of Campbell of Ardrishaig.

'Are you seeing anything, boys?' It was old Grant shouting from the doghouse, the wind whipping the words off his lips.

'There's nothing, Seumas,' Torry bawled back. 'Just nothing at all.'

I handed the spotlight, an ancient Aldis, over to Eachan and made my way aft. Seumas Grant, his hands light on the wheel, stood there quietly, his face a mask of blood – when yon great, seething comber had buried the *Dileas* and smashed in the window, he hadn't got out of the way quick enough.

But the old eyes were calm, steady, and watchful as ever.

'It's no good, Mr Grant,' I shouted at him. 'We'll never find anyone tonight, and nothing could have lived so long in this. It's hopeless, just hopeless – the *Dileas* can't last out much longer. We might as well go back.'

He said something. I couldn't catch it, and bent forward. 'I was just wondering,' he said, like a man in a muse, 'whether Lachie would have turned back.'

I backed slowly out of the wheelhouse, and I cursed Seumas Grant, I cursed him for that terrible love he bore for those two sons of his, for Donald Archie and Lachlan. And then – then I felt the shame, black and crawling, welling up inside me, and I cursed myself. Stumbling, I clawed my way for'ard again.

I was only halfway there when I heard Eachan shouting, his voice high and excited.

'There, Torry, look there! Just off the port bow. Somebody in the water – no, by God, two of them!'

When the *Dileas* heaved over the next crest, I looked along the beam of the Aldis. Eachan was right. There, sure enough, were two dark forms struggling in the water.

In three quick jumps I was back at the doghouse, pointing. Old Grant just nodded, and started edging the *Dileas* across. What a skill he had with him, that old one! Bring the bows too far round and we'd broach to and be gone in a second in yon great gullies between the waves. But old Seumas made never a mistake.

And then a miracle happened. Just that, Mr MacLean – a miracle. It was the Sea of Galilee all over again. Mind you, the waves were as terrible as ever, but just for a moment the wind dropped away to a deathly hush – and suddenly, off to starboard, a thin, high-pitched wail came keening out of the darkness.

In a flash, Torry had whipped his Aldis round, and the beam, plunging up and down, settled on a spot less than a hundred yards away – almost dead ahead. At first I thought it was just some wreckage, then I could see it was a couple of timber baulks and planks tied together. And lying on top of this makeshift raft – no, by God, *lashed* to it! – were a couple of children. We caught only flying glimpses of them: up one minute, down the next, play-things of the devil in yon madness of a sea. The poor wee souls. Oh Dhia! The poor wee souls.

'Mr Grant!' I roared in old Seumas's ear. 'There's a raft dead ahead – two wee children on it.'

The old eyes were quiet as ever. He just stared straight ahead: his face was like a stone.

'I canna be picking up both,' he said, his voice level and never a touch of feeling in it, damn his flinty heart. 'To come round in this would finish us – I'll have to quarter for the shelter of Seal Point to turn. Can the children be hanging on a while longer, do you think, Calum?'

'The children are near gone,' I said flatly. 'And they're not hanging on – they're *lashed* on.'

He looked quickly at me, his eyes narrowing.

'Lashed, did you say, Calum?' he asked softly. 'Lashed?'

I nodded without speaking. And then a strange thing happened, Mr MacLean, a strange thing indeed. Yon craggy old face of his broke into a smile – I can see yet the gleam of his teeth and the little rivers of blood running down his face – and he nodded several times as if in satisfaction and understanding . . . And he gave the wheel a wee bit spin to starboard.

The little raft was drifting down fast on us, and we had only the one chance of picking them up. But with old Seumas at the wheel that was enough, and Torry Mor, with one sweep of his great arm, had the children, raft and all, safely aboard.

We took them below and old Grant worked his way up to Seal Point. Then we came tearing down the Sound, steady as a rock – for in a heavy stern sea there's no boat on earth the equal of a Loch-Fyner – but never a trace of the two men did we see. A mile out from harbour old Seumas handed over to Torry Mor and came below to see the children.

They were sitting up on a bunk before the stove, wrapped in blankets – a lad of nine and a fair-haired wee lass of six. Pale, pale they were, and frightened and exhausted, but a good night's sleep would put them right.

Quietly I told old Grant what I'd learned. They'd been playing in a wee skiff, under the sheltered walls of the Buidhe harbour, when the

boy had gone too near the entrance and the wind
had plucked them out to the open Sound. But
they had been seen, and the two men had come
after them in the ferryboat: and then, they couldn't
turn back. The rest they couldn't remember: the
poor wee souls they'd been scared to death.

I was just finishing when Eachan came below.

'The wind's backing, Seumas, and the sea with
it. Perhaps there's a chance for yon two – if they're
swimmers at all – of being *carried ashore*.'

Old Seumas looked up. His face was tired, lined
and – all of a sudden – old.

'There's no chance, Eachan, no chance at all.'

'How can you be so sure, man?' Eachan argued.
'You never know.'

'I know, Eachan.' The old man's voice was a
murmur, a million miles away. 'I know indeed.
What was good enough for their old father was
good enough for Donal' and Lachie. I never learned
to swim – and neither did they.'

We were shocked into silence, I tell you. We
looked at him stupidly, unbelievingly, then in
horror.

'You mean –' I couldn't get the words out.

'It was Lachie and Donal' all right. I saw them.'
Old Grant gazed sightlessly into the fire. 'They
must have come back early from Scavaig.'

A whole minute passed before Eachan spoke,
his voice wondering, halting.

'But Seumas, Seumas! Your own two boys. How could you – '

For the first and only time old Grant's self-control snapped. He cut in, his voice low and fierce, his eyes masked with pain and tears.

'And what would you have had me do, Eachan? Pick them up and let these wee souls go?'

He went on, more slowly now.

'Can't you see, Eachan? They'd used the only bits of wood in yon old ferryboat to make a wee raft for the children. They knew what they were doing – and they knew, by doing it, that there was no hope for themselves. They did it deliberately, man. And if I hadn't picked the wee craturs up, it – it – '

His voice trailed off into silence, then we heard it again, the faintest shadow of a whisper.

'My two boys, Lachie and Donal' – oh, Eachan, Eachan, I couldna be letting them down.'

Old Grant straightened, reached out for a bit of waste, and wiped the blood from his face – and, I'm thinking, the tears from his eyes. Then he picked up the wee girl, all wrapped in her blankets, set her on his knee and smiled down gently.

'Well, now, mo ghaol, and how would you be fancying a wee drop hot cocoa?'

St George and the Dragon

If ever a man had a right to be happy, you would have thought it was George. In the eyes of any reasonable man, especially a parched and dusty city-dweller, George, at that very moment, was already halfway to Paradise.

Above, the hot afternoon sun beat down from a cloudless summer sky; on either side the golden stubble fields of the south slid lazily by; beneath his feet pulsed the sleek length of a 25-foot cabin cruiser; and immediately ahead stretched the lovely and unruffled reaches of the Lower Dipworth canal – not to mention the prospect of an entire month's vacation. Halfway to Paradise? The man was there already.

Dr George Rickaby, BSc, MSc, DS, AMIEE, considered himself the most unfortunate of mortals. How grossly deceived the world would be, he thought bitterly, if it judged by what it saw. What if he had sufficient money to indulge his taste for

inland cruising and plenty of time to enjoy it?
What if he had for his crew his devoted and indus-
trious ex-batman whose sole aim in life was to
prevent George from overexerting himself? What
if he was spoken of as a coming man in nuclear
fission? What, even, if the Minister of Supply had
been known to clap his shoulder and call him
George?

Dust and ashes, mused George disconsolately,
easing the cruiser round a wooded corner of the
canal, just dust and ashes. But he supposed he
shouldn't judge the foolish imaginings of an ignorant world too harshly. He mournfully regarded
the spotless deck of white pine. After all, in the
days of his youth, he had been criminally guilty of
the same thing himself. Why, only three months
ago –

'Look out! You're going to hit me!'

The high-pitched, urgent shout cut through
George's painful daydreams like a knife. He hurriedly straightened himself to the full height of his
painfully lean six feet, clutched at his spectacles
and blinked myopically ahead through his thick-
lensed glasses.

'Quickly, quickly, you idiot, or it'll be too late!'

George had a momentary impression of a barge,
its bows fast on the bank and blocking three-
quarters of the canal, and, in its stern, a noisy and
wildly gesticulating young female. All of this registered only superficially. George was not a man of

action and his upper centres were momentarily paralysed.

'Starboard, you fool, starboard your helm!' she yelled frantically.

George awoke to life and grabbed the wheel. But, as said, he was not a man of action. He was not at his best in emergencies. Spin the wheel he did, and with tremendous speed and energy. But he spun it in the wrong direction.

A mile away on the Upper Dipworth green, smock-coated octogenarians stirred uneasily in their sleep as the sound of the crash reverberated across the peaceful meadows. But in no time at all they were again sunk in peaceful slumber.

Back on the canal, however, matters showed every sign of taking a much more lively turn. The shock of the collision had flung the female bargee, in most unladylike mid-sentence, on to the bows of George's cruiser. At the same time, George had been catapulted forward. For the space of ten seconds they eyed each other malevolently from a distance of two feet.

The lady spoke first.

'Of all the bungling fools! Are you completely blind, you – you – you roadhog?' she demanded fiercely. 'Or perhaps, poor man – ' this in a tone of vitriolic sweetness – 'too much of the sun?' She tapped her head significantly.

George rose to his feet in a hurt and dignified silence. With this latest injustice his cup of bitterness was full to overflowing. But he had been brought up in a stern school. He hoped he knew how to behave like a gentleman.

'If either your boat or yourself is in any way damaged, please accept my apologies,' he said coldly. 'But you must admit it is unusual, to say the least of it, to see a barge sailing broadside up a canal. I mean, one doesn't expect that sort of thing – '

Here George suddenly broke off. He had adjusted his spectacles and now saw the lady clearly for the first time.

She was well worth looking at, George admitted to himself dispassionately. Burnished red hair, intensely blue – if unfriendly – eyes, long golden limbs, a sleeveless green sweater and very abbreviated white shorts – she had, he privately confessed, everything.

'Sailing broadside, you clown!' she snapped angrily, brushing aside his proffered hand and climbing painfully to her feet. 'Broadside, he says.' She flexed a speculative knee, while George stood by admiringly, and seemed relieved to find that it still worked.

'Can't you see I'm stuck right into the bank?' she enquired icily. 'It's just happened and I haven't had time to move. Why on earth couldn't you pass by my stern?'

'I'm sorry,' said George stiffly, 'but, after all, your boat is lying in a patch of shadow where these trees are. Besides – er – I wasn't paying much attention,' he concluded lamely.

'You certainly wasn't – I mean weren't,' retorted the redhead acidly. 'Of all the inept and panic-stricken displays – '

'Enough,' said George sternly. 'Not only was it your fault, but no damage has been done to your old barge anyway. But look at my bows!' he exclaimed bitterly.

The redhead tossed her head in a nice blend of scorn and indifference, swung round, picked her way delicately over the cruiser's splintered bows and buckled rails and gracefully stepped aboard the barge. George, after a moment's hesitation, followed her aboard.

She turned round quickly, stretching her hand out for the tiller, which lay conveniently near. To George, her hair seemed redder than ever. Her blue eyes almost sparked with anger.

'I don't remember inviting you aboard,' she said dangerously. 'Get off my barge.'

'I didn't invite you aboard either,' George pointed out reasonably. 'I have merely come,' he added loftily, 'to offer what assistance I can.'

She tightened her grip on the tiller. 'You have five seconds. I'm perfectly capable of looking after – '

'Look!' cried George excitedly. 'The tiller rope!' He picked up a loose end, neatly severed except for a broken strand. 'It's been cut.'

'What a brain,' remarked the lady caustically. 'Do you think the mice have been at it?'

'Very witty, very witty indeed. The point is, if it's been cut, somebody cut it. I don't suppose,' he added doubtfully, 'that you go about cutting tiller ropes.'

'No, I don't,' she replied bitterly. 'But Black Bart does. He'd cut anything. Tillers, mooring ropes, throats – they all come alike to him.'

'A thorough going villain, it would seem. Possibly you are biased. And who might Black Bart be?'

'Biased!' She struggled incoherently for words. 'Biased, he says. A man who robs my father, puts him in hospital, steals carriage contracts, sabotages barges. Right now he's on his way to the Totfield Granary to steal the summer contract from me. First come, first served.'

'Oh, come now,' said George peaceably. 'Piracy on the Lower Dipworth canal. In 1953, England and broad daylight. I am, I have been told, a more than normally gullible character – '

'Do you see any Navy around to prevent it?' she interrupted swiftly. 'Or any witnesses – this is the loneliest canal in England.'

George peered thoughtfully at her through his bifocals. 'You have a point there. Fortunately, you are not alone. Eric – my man – and I – '

'I'm too busy to laugh. I can take care of all this myself. Get off my boat.'

George was nettled. He forgot his well-bred upbringing.

'Now, look here, Ginger,' he burst out, 'I don't see why – '

'Did you call me "Ginger"?' she enquired sweetly.

'I did. As I was saying – '

Barely in time, he saw the tiller swinging round. He ducked, stumbled, clawed wildly at the air and fell backwards into the murky depths of the Lower Dipworth canal, clutching his precious bifocals in his left hand. When he surfaced, the redhead was no longer there, and in her place was the ever ready Eric, boathook in hand.

An hour later the cruiser was chugging along the canal at a respectful distance behind the barge. George, clad in a pair of immaculate tennis flannels and morosely watching his duck trousers and jersey flapping from the masthead, had once again fallen prey to his bitter thoughts.

Women, he brooded darkly, were the very devil. Three months previously he had been the happiest of men. And today – this very day was to have been his wedding day. The least his fiancée could have done, he considered, was to have switched her wedding date with the same ease and facility as she had switched prospective husbands.

But women had no finer feelings. Take this redhead, for instance, this termagant, this copper-headed Amazon, this female dragon in angel's clothing. Perfect confirmation of his belief in women's fundamental injustice, unfairness and lack of sensibility. Not that George needed any confirmation.

'Lock ahead, sir,' sang out Eric in the bows. 'And another boat.'

George squinted ahead into the setting sun. The redhead was steering her barge skilfully alongside the canal bank and, even as he watched, she jumped nimbly ashore, rope in hand, and made fast. Just beyond hers, another and much more ancient barge was gradually disappearing behind the lock gate. One gate was already shut, the other was being slowly closed by a burly individual who was pushing the massive gate handle. This, George guessed, might very possibly be Black Bart. The situation had interesting possibilities.

'Take her alongside, Eric, and tie up,' said George. 'The presence of a man of tact is called for up there, or I'm much mistaken.' With that, he leapt ashore and scrambled up the bank to the scene of conflict.

Conflict there undoubtedly was, but it was very one-sided. The man who had been pushing the gate shut, a very large, swarthy, unshaven and ugly customer with the face of a retired prize-fighter, continued to close it steadily, contemptuously fending off the redhead with one arm. Such blows as she landed had no effect at all. An elderly and obviously badly frightened lock-keeper hovered nervously in the background. He made no attempt to interfere.

'Now, now, Mary, me gal,' the prize-fighter was saying. 'Temper, temper. Assaulting a poor innocent feller like myself. Shockin', so it is. A criminal offence.'

'Leave that dock gate open, Jamieson,' she cried furiously. 'There's plenty of room for two barges, and you know it. Cutting people's tiller ropes! It'll cost me an hour if you go through alone. You – you villain.' The redhead was becoming a trifle confused. She struggled fiercely but to no effect at all.

'Language, language, my dear.' Bart grinned wickedly. 'And tiller ropes' – he started in large surprise – 'I don't know what you are talking about. As for letting your barge in . . . No-o-o.' He shook his head regretfully. 'I couldn't risk my paint.' He spat fondly in the direction of the battered hulk which lay in the dock below.

'Can I be of any assistance?' interrupted George.

'Beat it, Fancypants,' said Bart courteously.

'Oh, go away,' snapped the redhead.

'I will not go away. This is my business. This is everybody's business. An injustice is being done. Leave this to me.'

Jamieson paused in his efforts and regarded George under lowered eyebrows. George ignored him and turned to the redhead.

'Mary, me gal – er – I mean, Miss – why won't this ruffian let your barge into the lock?' he asked.

'Because, don't you see, it'll give him an hour's start on me. His barge is far older and slower. It's sixty miles to the Granary yet. He's determined to get there first, so he'll use any method to stop me.' Tears of rage welled up in her eyes.

George turned and faced Black Bart.

'Open that gate,' he commanded.

Bart's mouth fell open, just for a second, then tightened ominously.

'Run away, sonny,' he scoffed, 'I'm busy.'

George removed his yachting cap and placed it carefully on the ground.

'You leave me no alternative,' he stated. 'I shall have to use force.'

Mary clutched his arm. Her blue eyes were no longer hostile, but genuinely concerned.

'Please go away,' she pleaded. 'Please. You don't know him.'

'That's right. Oh please,' Bart mocked. 'Tell him what I did to your father.'

'Silence, woman,' George ordered. 'And hold these.'

He thrust his spectacles into her reluctant hand and swung round. Unfortunately, without his glasses, George literally could not distinguish a tramcar from a haystack. But he was too angry to care. His normal calm had completely vanished. He took a quick step forward and lashed out blindly at the place where Black Bart had been when last he had seen him.

But Black Bart was no longer there. He had thoughtfully moved quite some time previously. Further, and unfortunately for George, Black Bart had twenty-twenty vision and no finer feelings whatsoever. A murderous right whistled up and caught George one inch below his left ear. From the point of view of weight and the spirit in which given, it could be in no way compared to the encouraging clap he had so recently received from the Minister of Supply. George rose upwards and backwards, neatly cleared the edge of the lock and, for the second time in the space of an hour, described a graceful parabolic arc into the depths of the Lower Dipworth canal.

The girl, white-faced and trembling, stood motionless for a few seconds, then swung frantically round on Black Bart.

'You swine,' she cried. 'You vicious brute! You've killed him. Quickly, quickly – get him out! He'll drown, he'll drown!' The redhead was very close to tears.

Black Bart shrugged indifferently. 'I should worry,' he said callously. 'It's his own fault.'

Mary, colour returning to her cheeks, looked at him incredulously.

'But – but you did it! You knocked him in. I saw you.'

'Self-defence,' explained Black Bart carefully. 'I only stumbled against him.' He smiled slowly, evilly. 'Besides, I can't swim.'

Seconds later, another splash broke the stillness of the summer evening. The lady had gone to the rescue of her rescuer.

'Get off my barge,' she ordered angrily. 'I don't want your help.'

George seated himself more comfortably on the counter of the barge and peacefully surveyed the wooden jetty where the three boats had tied up for the night. He appeared none the worse for the accident of a couple of hours earlier.

'I will not get off,' said George, calmly puffing at his pipe. 'And neither,' he added, 'will Eric.' He indicated his companion who then engaged in viewing the night sky through the bottom of an upturned tankard. 'Every young lady – especially a young lady struggling to carry on her father's business – needs protection. Eric and I will look after you.'

'Protection!' she scoffed bitterly. 'Protection!' George followed her meaningful glance towards the white shorts and green jersey on the line. They were still dripping. 'You couldn't take care of a wheelbarrow. Can't sail, can't swim, can't defend yourself – a fine protector you'd make.' She breathed deaply and with fearful restraint. 'Get off!'

''Ere, 'ere, Miss,' said the aggrieved Eric, 'that's not quite fair. The guv'nor's no sissy. 'E's got a medal, 'e 'as.'

'What did he get it for?' she queried acidly. 'Ballroom dancing?'

'The lady, I'm afraid, Eric, is annoyed,' said George. 'Perhaps justifiably so. All dragons,' he muttered under his breath, 'are in a state of perpetual annoyance.'

'What was that?' the lady demanded sharply.

'Nothing,' said George, courteously but firmly. 'You will now please retire to your bed. No further harm will befall you or your boat. Eric and I,' he finished poetically, 'will watch over you to the break of day.'

Mary made as if to protest, hesitated, shrugged her shoulders resignedly, and turned away.

'Suit yourself,' she said indifferently. 'Perhaps,' she added hopefully, 'you'll both catch pneumonia.'

For some time, there followed sounds of movement in the cabin, then the light was switched off. By and by the sound of deep and peaceful slumber drifted up the companionway. It was in many ways a pleasant sound – infinitely so, indeed, in comparison with the obligato of snores already issuing from the two faithful watchers in the stern.

Sleep, however, was not universal. Far from it. Black Bart and his henchman were not only awake, but uncommonly active. The latter had stealthily vanished into the engine room of George's cruiser: Black Bart himself was squatting on one of the submerged cross-beams bracing the piers of the jetty. Looped over his shoulder were about sixty feet of slender wire hawser. One end was secured to the pier, the other to the rudder of the barge, immediately below the sleeping warriors. The coils he let fall gently to the bottom of the canal.

At 7.00 a.m. the following morning, George and Eric left the barge in a hurry. The frying pan wielded by the redhead was daunting enough, but far more devastating were her scorn and derision.

At 7.30 Black Bart's barge moved off, chugged along the canal for a couple of hundred yards, then stopped. Jamieson wanted a grandstand view of the proceedings.

At 8.00 a.m., Eric appeared on deck, luridly cursing the villain who had drained all the paraffin tanks and refilled them with water.

At 8.02 George made his hurried way along the bank to Mary's boat in urgent search of fuel. He was driven off by unkind words and a bargepole.

At 8.05, Mary cast off, and at 8.06, with a terrific rending, splintering noise, the rudder was torn off. Immediately the barge slewed round and thudded into the bank.

At 8.08, George had run along the towpath and leapt aboard to offer help. At 8.09 the redhead knocked him into the canal and at 8.10 she fished him out again.

Two hundred yards away, Black Bart was bent double, convulsed at the results of his own genius. Finally he straightened up, wiped the streaming tears from his eyes, and journeyed on towards the famous Watman's Folly, the last stopover of the trip.

'Ol' man, I've mishjudged you – mishjudged you badly, ol' man. Sorry, Bart, ol' man. But you unnershtand how it is. Women! Women! Tchah! Did you see what she did to me? Eh? Did you see it?' George was incoherent with indignation.

'Sure, sure, Doc, I saw it.' Black Bart swore fluently. 'She's a bad-tempered young lady.' 'Lady' was not Bart's choice of word. 'Better rid of her. Sorry about the scrap at the lock, Doc. All her fault, the wicked little so-and-so.'

'It's forgotten, Bart, ol' man, forgotten. All my own fault. Pals, eh, ol' man?'

The new-found pals solemnly shook hands, then returned to the serious competitive business of deplenishing the Watman's Arms available supplies of West Country cider. It was powerful stuff. George appeared to be winning by a short head: but then George was pouring nearly all of his into a convenient window box. Black Bart remained happily unaware of this. He was likewise ignorant of the immense care with which George had arranged this accidental meeting – the Arms was a favourite haunt of Jamieson's. Striking up an acquaintanceship on a friendly basis had been easy – after what Black Bart had seen that morning, George's friendliness came as no surprise. Besides, George was spending very freely.

' 'S ten o'clock, Doc,' said Bart warningly. 'Chucking-out time, you know.'

'Imposhible, ol' man,' replied George thickly. 'We've only been here ten minutes. Tell you what, ol' man,' he continued eagerly. 'Lesh make a night of it. Eh? ol' pal? Come on.'

Ten minutes later the old pals were staggering erratically along the towpath, singing in what they frequently praised as wonderful harmony, and swinging a demijohn of cider in either hand. First they passed the cruiser, then Mary's barge with the jury-rigged rudder – Bart meant to attend to that later on – and finally boarded Bart's barge.

Bart's barge lay close by Watman's Folly, which was only ten miles short of the Granary. The Folly was what is known as a blind lock. It had lock gates at either end, but the outer end led nowhere. It just stopped there, overlooking the Upper Totfield valley – an embryo canal killed by finance. Like most blind locks, it had been sealed by concrete.

Bart's henchman welcomed them eagerly, and the night's festivities really commenced. At half past one the henchman slid beneath the table. At a quarter to two George followed him, and at two o'clock Bart, in the act of draining the last demijohn, crashed to the floor in a highly spectacular fashion.

George rose briskly to his feet, dusted down his clothes and strode ashore. First, he boarded Mary's barge and rapped imperatively on her door.

A light immediately flicked on and in ten seconds a tousled red head and sleepy, rather scared blue eyes peeped round the door. When she saw who it was her expression changed to something curiously like gladness, then merely to relief, finally to exasperation.

'I know, I know,' said George. '"Get off my barge". Well, I'm just going. I am not,' he added hastily, 'keeping a watch over you tonight. Just came to tell you to be prepared to move early tomorrow. I don't think Black Bart will be feeling particularly friendly towards any of us in a few hours' time.'

'What are you talking about,' she asked wonderingly. 'And just what do you propose to do?' she inquired suspiciously.

'Wait and see,' said George ungallantly. 'Perhaps I'm no sailor, swimmer or boxer but – ' he tapped himself briefly on the forehead – 'possibly I am not completely useless in every department. Goodnight.'

He returned to his cruiser, collected Eric, and together they made their way back to Bart's barge. They unhitched his mooring ropes, dragged the barge along the canal, opened the gates of the Folly, creaky and stiff with long disuse, and towed the barge inside. Once they had it safely inside, they closed the gates and George, producing a hacksaw, thoughtfully sawed off the handle of the sluice trap, so that it could not be opened to admit water.

While he was doing this, Eric was struggling with the sluice trap at the blind end. Together they raised it and immediately the water rushed out in a continuous jet. They then sawed that handle off, so that it could no longer be closed. In ten minutes the lock was empty, and the barge, with its unconscious crew, was high and dry and fast in the mud. Black Bart and his barge were there for some time to come.

In the end, it was touch and go. The scheme had worked perfectly, but its author almost came to a sticky and premature end.

George had underestimated Black Bart's terrific powers of recuperation. All were awake early next morning and at seven o'clock, just as George was casting off Mary's ropes, Black Bart, bloodshot and unshaven, covered from head to foot in mud, slime and grease, appeared over the top of Watman's Folly like some savage prehistoric monster. Nor did the resemblance stop there. Black Bart was out for blood.

George had no time to reach his own boat, which was just moving off. Cursing and raving like a madman, Black Bart leapt in tigerishly, his great fists swinging in blind anger. But his own speed and power robbed him of revenge. A tremendous blow caught George on the shoulder, spun him round like a top, and knocked him head first into the canal for the fourth time in thirty-six hours.

George struggled wildly in the water, his arms windmilling frantically, spluttering, coughing, going under and resurfacing at regular intervals. But there was no real cause for worry. For a third time a slim vision in red, brown and white sliced down through the waters of the canal and towed the feebly struggling George towards the barge. Eric helped them aboard.

Ten minutes had passed and still George had not recovered. With Black Bart safely half-a-mile behind, still cursing fearfully, George was in no hurry to recover. His head was pillowed on Mary's lap; a very comfortable pillow he thought. Besides, he could hear his own cruiser purring alongside and he did not feel like meeting Eric's accusing eye.

He stirred, experimentally, and his eyebrows fluttered open. The redhead still sat motionless on the deck, oblivious of her soaking clothes, mechanically steering with one hand. She was whispering, 'George, George, oh George' in a manner highly pleasing to George's ears: and her blue eyes, usually so hostile and snapping, were now misted over with an anxiety and a soft concern.

But, he thought in a delicious drowsiness, I must remember to warn Eric about the medal. Mary must never know – well, at least not till later. For George really was the holder of nothing less than the George Medal. It had been given him for an amazing feat of personal survival when his fighter had crashed in the Mediterranean, eight miles off the Libyan coast. He had been wounded, dazed, weak from the loss of blood and he ought to have died. But George had reached land.

And he had swum every foot of the way.

The Arandora Star

The *Arandora Star* had indeed fallen upon evil days. Less than a year had elapsed since the ending of her great days, the proud days when the fluttering of the Blue Star house flag at her masthead had signalled in a score of harbours all over the world the stately arrival of one of the elite of the British Mercantile Marine – a luxury cruise liner on her serene and regal way round the better ports of the seven seas.

Less than a year had elapsed since she had taken aboard her last complement of financially select passengers, wrapped them in a silken cocoon of luxury and impeccable service and transported them painlessly north to the Norwegian fjords in search of the summer sun or south to bask in the warmth of the blue Caribbean skies. Deck games, soft music, cinema shows, dancing to the ship's band, the tinkling of ice in tall frosted glasses, the unobtrusive but omnipresent white-jacketed stewards – there had been no lack of every last comfort and convenience which might in any way conduce to the perfect shipboard holiday atmosphere of relaxation and romance.

Less than a year had elapsed, but now all that was gone. The change was great. The relaxation and romance were no more. Neither were the bands, the bars, the deck games, the dancing under the stars.

Greater even was the change in the ship itself. The hull, upper-works and funnel that had once so gaily reflected their colours in the millpond waters of fjords and Mediterranean ports were now covered in a dull coat of neutral grey. The public rooms had been stripped of their expensive furnishings, panelling and draperies, cabins and staterooms altered and fitted with crude metal bunks to accommodate twice – and in some cases four times – as many passengers as formerly.

But the greatest change of all was in the nature of the passengers, and the purpose of their voyage. Where once there had been a few hundred affluent Britons, there were now no fewer than 1,600 far from affluent German and Italian internees and prisoners of war: and they were going not in search of the sun, but to internment camps in Canada for the duration of the war.

These internees, composed mostly of British-resident civilians and captured German seamen, were the lucky ones. They were leaving the bleak austerity of blacked-out and rationed England for the comfort and comparative plenty of North America. True, they were going to be locked up and guarded for months or even years, and it was going to be a dull and boring war for them: but at least they would be well clad, well fed – and above all safe.

Or they would have been. Unfortunately, both for the Germans and their Italian allies, soon after 6.00 a.m. on 2 July, 1940, on their second day out from Liverpool and some way off the west coast of Ireland, the *Arandora Star* slowly swam into view, and framed herself on the crossed hairs of the periscope sights of a German U-boat's captain.

The torpedo struck the *Arandora Star* fair and square amidships, erupting in a roar of sound and a towering wall of white water that cascaded down on the superstructure and upper decks, blasting its way through the unarmoured ship's side clear into the engine room. Deep inside the ship, transverse watertight bulkheads buckled and split under the impact, and the hundreds of tons of water, rushing in through the great jagged rent torn in the ship's side, flooded fore and aft with frightening speed as if goaded by some animistic savagery and bent on engulfing and drowning trapped men before they could fight their way clear and up to freedom.

Many of the crew died in these first few moments before they had recovered from the sheer

physical shock of the explosion, their first intima-
tion of the direction in which danger lay being a
tidal wave of seething white and oil-streaked water
bearing down upon them even as their numbed
minds registered the certain knowledge that the
one and only brief moment in which they could
have rushed for safety was gone forever.

From the already flooded depths of the ship
some few did manage to claw their way up iron
ladders and companionways to the safety of the
upper deck, to join the hundreds already there:
but they had no sooner arrived than it was swiftly
borne in upon them that this safety was an illu-
sion, that their chances of being able to get clear
away of the already sinking liner were indeed
remote.

In the reports of the tragedy which appeared in
the British press on Thursday, 4 July and Friday, 5
July, there was a remarkable degree of unanimity
with regard to what constituted the reasons for
the subsequent appalling loss of life. Not reasons,
rather, but one single all-encompassing reason:
the unbelievable cowardliness and selfishness of
the Germans and the Italians who, grouping
themselves on an ugly nationalistic basis, fought
desperately for precedence in the boats, with the
inevitable result that the speed and orderliness
which the rapid loading and lowering of the
lifeboats demanded were utterly impossible.

The press reports of the time leave one in no doubt as to that. 'Casualties due to panic': 'Passengers fight to reach boats': 'Fights among aliens' and similar uncompromising captions headlined articles which spoke freely of disgraceful panic, of the wild rushes and cowardice of the Germans – 'great hulking brutes kicking and punching every person who got in their way' – who fought to get into the boats, of the sickening scramble of the Italians who thought of nothing but their own skins, of scores of people being forced overboard, of British soldiers and sailors losing invaluable time, and often their own lives, in separating the madly fighting, screaming aliens.

One report even had the Italians so crazy with fear that they fought not the Germans but among themselves; thirty of them, it was alleged, battling furiously for the privilege of sliding down a single rope.

In order to establish, among other things, just how widespread and uncontrollable this panic had been, survivors of the *Arandora Star* were recently interviewed and four of these finally selected as providing testimony as impeccable as we are ever likely to have. They were selected on the bases (a) that they represented different contingents – crew, guards and internees – aboard the ship and (b) that their independently volunteered statements were mutually corroborative to a very high degree indeed. Such insignificant discrepancies as existed were readily accounted for by the fact that they were in different parts of the ship and all left it by different means.

These four are: Mr Sidney ('Nobby') Fulford, ship's barman, of 57 Northbrook Road, Southampton: Mr Edward ('Ted') Crisp of 210 High Road, North Weald, Essex, a veteran Blue Star Line steward who has been going to sea for 39 years: Mr Mario Zampi, the well-known Italian-born film producer of Wardour Street: and Mr Ivor Duxberry, a War Department employee, of 89 Johnson Road, Heston, Middlesex.

In view of the newspaper reports of the time, their answers to the question of the extent of the panic and pitched battles which are alleged to have taken place are singularly interesting.

'I saw no signs of panic and no fighting whatsoever,' Mr Fulford states flatly: and as sixty internees left the *Arandora Star* in the same boat as he, he should have had an excellent chance to observe anything of the kind. 'There was confusion, of course, but only that.'

Mr Crisp said exactly the same.

Mr Zampi agreed. 'These reports of panic and disorder among the internees were just not true. The only trouble I saw was between a British Army sergeant and his men: they had jumped into a lifeboat and shots were fired at them to make them leave.'

This statement by Mr Zampi, who must have suffered considerably on hearing the courage of his countrymen so frequently maligned in the days after the sinking, might well be suspected of being actuated by pique, nationalistic bias, or a very understandable desire to get a little of his own back, especially as it seems so grossly improbable.

In point of fact it is perfectly true, except that it was a corporal Mr Zampi saw and not a sergeant: and that corporal, by a remarkable coincidence, was the fourth witness, then Corporal Duxberry of the Welsh Regiment, the most informative of all the witnesses, whose phenomenal memory is matched only by the detailed accuracy of his recollections of these days.

'Some of the guard,' Ivor Duxberry says, 'disregarded the order of "Prisoners of war and internees first into the boats". Major Bethell – CO of the 109 POW unit – using a megaphone from the bridge, ordered them out. When they didn't respond, he ordered me to fire a volley over their heads to show that he meant business.' Duxberry fired as ordered, and the soldiers soon left.

Duxberry confirms that there was no general panic or fighting. He did, he says, see two Italians, a young man and an old, fighting for a position in a boat, a fight which quickly ended when a German internee knocked out the younger man with a ship's dry scrubber and escorted the old man into the boat.

Apart from these minor incidents, there was no trouble at all of the kind described in the papers at the time. Why, then, these reports?

The obvious answer, of course, is that the citizens of an embattled nation tend to become afflicted with an irremediable chauvinism, a nationalistic myopia which only peace can cure, a temporary suspension of reasonable judgment where our side, our troops, become the good, the kindly, the brave, while those of the other, the enemy, become the bad, the wicked and the cowardly.

But, as so often, the obvious answer is the wrong one. Top newspapermen, such as covered these stories, are, as a class, less likely to be affected by such unthinking emotionalism than almost any other people. Hard-headed realists, cynics in the best sense of the word, they tend to regard with a very jaundiced eye indeed the flag-waving, drum-beating, nonsensically juvenile jingoism of the average nation at war. Their job is to get and evaluate facts.

It is more than likely that they did get and evaluate the facts, took a good look at them and hastily put them away, using instead the accounts of a few ill-informed survivors to put flesh on the bones of their stories and at the same time give a reasonable explanation for the dreadful loss of life. They did so because they had a very healthy fear of editors, of the censor and of the terms of imprisonment which might all too easily come the way of any man so foolish as to tell the truth in wartime, if that truth could be interpreted as a violation of security, as lowering morale or giving aid and encouragement to the enemy.

These are the facts, the true reasons for the great loss of life:

1. The ship was grossly overloaded. All the survivors agree on this. Originally – in peacetime – the *Arandora Star* carried 250 first-class passengers, but later had superstructure alterations made to accommodate another 200 passengers. On the morning of the disaster there were close on 1,700 internees and guards aboard, in addition to the normal ship's crew.

Ivor Duxberry was with his CO, Major Bethell, when the latter was told by the ship's master – Captain E. W. Moulton – that he had protested most strongly about the danger of overcrowding, and demanded that his number of passengers be cut by half. The authorities had refused to listen to him. It is not known precisely who these authorities were, except that they were *not* Frederick Leyland & Co, the owners of the vessel, nor the Blue Star Line, its managers.

2. Some of the survivors state that there were not enough lifejackets. The truth of this statement is difficult to substantiate – obviously no person, other than the chief officer and those directly responsible to him, can know where every

lifejacket is – but what seems beyond dispute is that if there were enough, they were not issued to all.

Many people drowned through the lack of these jackets. It may be, although it seems extremely unlikely, that scores of people forgot that they had these jackets: apart from that, many had none in the first place. Steward Crisp had no lifejacket, and neither had Corporal Duxberry, who says that, as far as he knows, not one member of the guard was issued with a lifejacket. Reports at the time speak of army officers handing over their lifejackets to internees, but these were isolated instances.

3. There were far too few lifeboats. There were about a dozen of these, old, worn out, and with a capacity of about sixty each, altogether a total capacity of less than half of the entire complement of the *Arandora Star*. Some of these had had oars, emergency provisions and plugs removed, to immobilize them against any escape attempt on the part of the internees. How those responsible for this monstrous action thought that any party of internees could steal a lifeboat with armed soldiers constantly on guard and sailors on lookout is difficult to understand: but it is downright impossible to understand how it could be thought possible to lower a boat safely in darkness with the liner racing at full speed through the rough Atlantic seas. It is hard to imagine any naval man being responsible for this action.

4. There appears to have been no lifeboat drill whatsoever. Neither Mr Crisp nor Mr Fulford had anything to say on this matter, very possibly and understandably because they wished to cast no reflection on their employers, one of the world's most respected shipping companies – an admirable but unnecessary reticence because no blame attaches to the company. But neither Mr Zampi nor Mr Duxberry had any such hesitations, and the absence of drill is borne out in Mr Lafitte's book *The Internment of Aliens*.

It would be easy, and perhaps proper, to call this criminal negligence, but, in fairness, it must be borne in mind that there were many confirmed Nazi merchant sailors and submariners on board who might have chosen the confusion of this drill as a cover to gain control of the ship.

5. The rafts, which might have saved most of those who could find no room in the lifeboats, were secured by wire. These wires could only be loosened by special implements which all too often were unobtainable, or their location unknown. Most of the rafts, immovably lashed in position, eventually went down with the *Arandora Star*.

6. All the above reasons – the overloading, shortage of lifejackets and lifeboats, the lack of drill and jammed rafts – undoubtedly contributed materially to the heavy loss of life. But, nevertheless, all of these taken together did not even begin to equal the lethal, murderous effect of one other

item, the existence of which was not even admitted at the time: barbed wire.

The decks of the ship were unrecognizable, surrounded and festooned with impenetrable barbed-wire fencing which turned the *Arandora Star* into a floating concentration camp.

'I had had a lot of experience with POW cages,' Ivor Duxberry says, 'but I have never seen barbed wire erected more expertly than this. It was impregnable – so closely woven that no space was big enough for a man to get his head through without damaging himself.

'This barbed wire partitioned the decks – *and cut off access to the lifeboats.*'

It cut off access to the lifeboats. One single damning statement that holds the key to the tragedy of the *Arandora Star* – barbed wire cut off access to the lifeboats. Little wonder, indeed, that security clamped down on all mention of this: what magnificent propaganda material it would have made for the Axis!

It is difficult indeed to understand why the omniscient authorities of the time deemed this murderous wire necessary – did they expect, perhaps, to prevent some of the internees from escaping by diving overboard in mid-Atlantic and swimming for the nearest continent? – but it is not difficult to understand the attitude of Captain Moulton who protested with the utmost violence against the erection of this wire.

'You are sending men to their deaths,' he
insisted, 'men who have sailed with me for many
years. If anything happens to the ship, that wire
will obstruct passage to the boats and rafts. We
shall be drowned like rats and the *Arandora Star*
turned into a floating deathtrap.'

But the authorities knew better than the man
who had spent a lifetime at sea. The barbed wire
remained. And the *Arandora Star* became a floating deathtrap.

That, then, was the desperate situation that con-
fronted all those who finally managed to struggle
to the upper deck. But not all of those who survived the initial impact of the explosion or the
lethal onrush of the invading waters reached the
upper deck.

There were old men aboard, old men and sick
men, and many of these never left their cabins –
they had been asleep in their bunks when the torpedo struck, and many of them died there. Others
were too weak to fight their way along flooded
alleys, or took wrong turnings in the Stygian darkness of the great liner's vast complex of passage-
ways: Edward Crisp owes his life simply to the fact
that he knew the internal geography of the ship
like the back of his hand.

Others again *did* reach the upper decks, found
their way to the nearest fore or aft lifeboat blocked
by rolls of athwartships barbed wire, and went

below again to find some passage which would bring them up to a lifeboat no further away than twenty yards from where they stood. But the press and confusion below decks was increasing steadily, the level of the water was rising, and many of those who went below were never seen again.

Major Bethell, OC of the guard, ordered his men to clear away the barbed wire in front of the lifeboats. (It appears that there was some method of loosening sections of the barbed barricade by operating a slipwire, but no instructions had been given in this.) The guard tore at the wire with rifles and bayonets – Ivor Duxberry has still the scars on his arms as the grim proof of his story – and the rush for the boats was on.

Unfortunately, because of the obstructing wire, trained members of the ship's company were not able to reach all their boats' positions – or at least not in time. Edward Crisp and Taffy Williams – the bosun's mate – arrived at their station to find sixty Germans and Italians already sitting in a lifeboat, and had to order them out – no easy task when everyone was convinced that the *Arandora Star* was already foundering – before they could begin to lower the boat. Elsewhere, some of the internees tried to lower the boats themselves and within a few minutes, in Duxberry's graphic phrase, half a dozen of them were hanging on one fall like turkeys outside a poulterer's shop.

But some of the prisoners of war, as distinct from the internees, proved invaluable. One such was Captain Burfend, master of the *Adolph Woermann*, who marched a group of men – for the most part highly experienced seamen and confirmed Nazis – in a column of two on to the boatdeck, and lowered several lifeboats in perfect order. Nazis or not, their behaviour was all that could have been wished for at this moment of crisis. Especially was this true of Captain Burfend himself. When he had seen as many men as possible, regardless of race, into the lifeboats for which he had assumed temporary responsibility, he denied himself a place in any of these, stepped back and went down with the *Arandora Star*.

But though there were not enough lifeboats for all, this was not realized. Most of the intervening barbed wire was still in position, with men flinging themselves bodily upon it, trying to tear it apart with their bare hands, only to find within seconds that they were caught beyond any hope of escape. Others smashed a path through with fire hydrants, went back, incredibly, to collect their suitcases, and returned to find the lifeboats gone.

The survivors, of course, were those who were not caught in or trapped by the barbed wire. Mario Zampi, who had lowered a raft only to have it taken over by some of his fellow countrymen already in the water, dived over the side and all but broke his neck when his lifejacket struck the water. Fulford jumped from the boatdeck – a dive at which even an Olympic champion would have baulked – and struck the water far beneath with such force that large quantities of oil and salt water were forced into his stomach and lungs: he, too, was injured by his lifejacket. Edward Crisp, as said, managed to get away in a lifeboat, while Ivor Duxberry slithered down a rope and landed astride the upturned hull of a lifeboat.

Even as the great liner foundered, there were hundreds still aboard. Most of these were trapped. Some were too terrified to jump. Others, like Captains Moulton and Burfend, elected to remain with the ship rather than abandon it before everyone else had been saved. Few of the regimental guard officers survived. When last seen, they were lined up, as one survivor put it, and chatting amiably like suburban passengers waiting in a morning bus queue. It is difficult to recognize either the wisdom or necessity of this quixotism and nonchalant acceptance of a fate which, until they themselves made the decision, had been by no means certain: but it is impossible not to admire their selfless gallantry.

At 7.30 a.m. the *Arandora Star* heeled over sharply until she was almost on her side in the water, the guard rails far below the surface of the sea, hesitated for a moment, then, momentarily shrouded in clouds of hissing steam, slid quietly beneath the surface of the Atlantic.

The waters in the immediate vicinity of the foundering liner were alive with people on rafts or clinging to planks or nonswimmers frantically churning the surface of the sea with the last of their rapidly failing strength. All saw what was coming, all struggled fearfully, desperately to avoid it, but for all but a few the effort had come too late, a meaningless tribute to the age-old instinct to survive. How many people were sucked down in the vortex of the plummeting *Arandora Star* will never be known: but no more, it is certain, than were dragged down, trapped by the impenetrable barrier of barbed wire, or still impaled on the savage hooks, helpless flies trapped in this monstrous spider's web.

The *Arandora Star* was gone, but almost a thousand of its passengers, guards and crew – mainly Italians and Germans – still lived, scattered in groups or singly over several square miles of the Atlantic. That morning the Atlantic, mercifully, was calm and all but windless – but the sea was bitterly cold. Before long the number of swimmers and those supported only by planks and benches became pitifully fewer and fewer. Mario Zampi lost all but one of the six companions who originally clung to the same bench as he. Their pathetic cries of 'Mother', repeated over and over again in three or four languages, grew fainter and fainter and gradually faded away altogether as the numbing cold struck through the scanty clothing and pathetically limited defences of the old, the infirm and the gravely wounded, and stopped the beating of their hearts. And some there were, supported by their life jackets, who, by and by, just lay face down in the water, dead.

About noon, a Sunderland flying boat appeared and circled the area dropping all it had in the way of first-aid kits, emergency rations, chocolate and cigarettes, and then disappeared to guide the Canadian destroyer *St Laurent* to the scene.

All of the survivors are unanimous in their unstinted praise of the magnificently selfless work performed by the crew of that ship: operating from the *St Laurent*'s boats while the destroyer itself kept constantly on the move to avoid submarines, they scoured the area for hours until they collapsed unconscious over their oars, having driven themselves far beyond the limits of exhaustion.

In all, the crew of the *St Laurent* picked up and took to safety over eight hundred survivors, an astonishing feat almost without parallel in the life-saving annals of the sea, almost enough to make one forget, if even only for a moment, the barbed wire and the thousand men who died.

Almost, but not quite.

Rawalpindi

Even with the two brand new untried battle cruisers under his command, even although he was
leading them on this, their first sortie against the
enemy and the cold, dark hostility of the winter
north Atlantic, Vice-Admiral Marschall was as
unworried as any fleet commander can ever hope
to be in wartime. Wilhelmshaven was dropping
south behind him into the early gathering dusk of
a November afternoon and the low flat shores of
Jede Bay were already vanishing into nothing-
ness, but Marschall never spared them a glance.
He was busy, far too busy for any of this nonsense
of sentimental farewells, and, besides, he knew he
didn't have to bother. Barring accidents, it would
only be a matter of brief time before he saw these
shores again.

And there would be no accidents. Of that the
Squadron Commander, Marschall, was convinced.
One of Germany's best and most experienced

naval officers, Vice-Admiral Marschall was fully
aware that in wartime the element of risk could
never be fully eliminated, that chance must
always play its part. But the risk was negligible:
not only was he the gambler who had been dealt
all the best cards in the pack – he was playing
against a blindfolded opponent.

Already, in these first few months of war, the
German Naval Intelligence Service, with the inten-
sive preparations of years behind them, was operating at maximum efficiency. Its agents were scattered
all over Britain and the neutral countries of Western
Europe – and these agents were the best there were.
The accuracy and completeness of the information
obtained was matched only by the speed with
which this information was transmitted to Berlin.

German Naval HQ knew the position, speed,
course and destination of almost every convoy leaving or approaching Britain. They knew the position
of every British capital ship – and they knew that on
that day, 21 November, 1939, every British capital
ship was either in harbour or in far distant waters:
that the *Nelson* and the *Rodney* were in the Clyde,
the *Hood* and the French battlecruiser *Dunkerque*
were in Plymouth, a cruiser squadron was fuelling
and victualling in Rosyth, and that the only other
ship they might have had to fear, the aircraft carrier
Furious was in Nova Scotia with the battleship
Repulse. They knew, too, that after the torpedoing of
the *Royal Oak* in Scapa Flow by Leutnant-Kapitän

Günther Prien's U-boat, the British Navy had pre-
cipitately abandoned that far northern base, and
retreated to the Clyde and Forth, maintaining only
a small secret base in Loch Ewe, a northwesterly
Scottish fjord. At least it was secret as far as the
British public and most of the Royal Navy were concerned: the Germans knew all about it.

There was, of course, no guarantee that these
ships would remain where they were. Again, the
Germans were unworried. Their experts had completely broken the British naval codes at that time,
with the results that British naval redisposition
orders were known to the Germans almost as
quickly as they were to the captains of the ships
concerned.

Not that Marschall had any intention of engag-
ing any large British ships in any case. His superior, Admiral Raeder, had been adamant on this
point. This was only a shakedown cruise which
might pay the added dividends of dislocating our
shipping and drawing off our patrols.

There was the further possibility that news of
the departure of the squadron might be transmitted to London by espionage agents, but, in view of
past achievements of the British Intelligence
Service, that was highly unlikely. At the time, our
Intelligence Service was untrained, cumbersome,
and almost wholly ineffectual – the *Deutschland*,
for instance, after her first Atlantic foray, had been
back in the Baltic for over a month before we

knew anything about it. And, it must be confessed, our sketchy air patrols over the North Sea
were, at the time, not much better than our
Intelligence Service.

Vice-Admiral Marschall, therefore, felt justifiably light of heart as his two battle cruisers, the
Scharnhorst and the *Gneisenau* cleared Jede Bay
and sailed out into the cold, wind-swept darkness
of the North Sea. A bitter night, a bad night, but
Marschall welcomed it, for over and above all the
cards he held in his hand, the darkness of the long
northern winter nights, the forecasted bad
weather and visibility reducing rain-squalls and
fog were further powerful allies, that made for
safety. Marschall reckoned that it would take him
exactly forty-eight hours to reach the Iceland–
Orkney line of the British contraband control.

The British Northern Patrols were in position,
thinly stretched out over nearly a thousand miles
of sea. Cruisers were the backbone of this patrol,
but mostly superannuated ships of the old C and D
classes. Only four ships could be reckoned as really
effective fighting units: the *Norfolk* and the *Suffolk*,
the same two ships as were to report the historic
breakthrough of the *Bismarck* into the Atlantic in
May 1941, were in exactly the same position as
they were on that memorable day – the Denmark
Strait – the *Glasgow* was just to the north-east of
the Shetlands, with the *Newcastle* stiffening the line

between the Faroes and Iceland. Of these, only the *Newcastle* was anywhere near the coming scene of action, but even she was too far away.

Holding much of the line in between these cruisers were the armed merchant ships. For contraband control – the stopping and searching of ships carrying proscribed cargoes – these ships were ideal in the high wild latitudes of the Atlantic. Big ex-passenger ships, able to remain at sea for long periods in bad weather, they were stripped of all their luxury fittings, and fitted with guns sufficient to deal with any cargo ship. But only with cargo ships – they were never intended to cope with anything else: it is significant that the very first move of the Admiralty when they finally learnt of the breakthrough of the *Scharnhorst* and *Gneisenau*, was to withdraw all the armed merchant ships off the northern patrol. But the order came too late, tragically but inevitably, for one of these ships; for it was not until the *Scharnhorst* and *Gneisenau* turned their great guns on the *Rawalpindi* that the Admiralty knew that these two ships, then the most powerful in the German Navy, were loose in the Atlantic.

The 17,000-ton *Rawalpindi*, in peacetime a crack P & O liner plying between Britain and the Far East, was one of the first Merchant Navy vessels to be converted to an armed merchant ship. Her gay pre-war colours were gone, lost under a drab coat of battleship grey. The lavishly furnished interior had been gutted, a main control gunnery room constructed and deck fittings removed to make way for ammunition lockers and her hastily installed armament – eight old 6-inch guns, four ranged along either side. But there had been no time, no opportunity to make any alteration to her unarmoured sides and decks, and the strengthening of these was largely impossible anyway: in terms of the penetrating power of modern armour-piercing shells, the hull of the *Rawalpindi* might as well have been made of paper.

The crew of the *Rawalpindi* knew this, but just accepted it, with the mental equivalent of a philosophic shrug, as just another of the hazards of the sea. Among the 280 officers and men aboard, there was not one to whom the sea and all its dangers were unknown, for in terms of experience if not in actual age – but more often than not in age as well – it was a crew of old men. Apart from fifty-odd officers and men who had served with the *Rawalpindi* as a regular passenger liner, the entire crew was composed of RNVR men of the Merchant Navy. RNVR – civilians with the bare essentials of naval training – reservists, and pensioners who had come back to the sea after having already completed twenty-two years in the Navy. There was not one active service officer or rating aboard the *Rawalpindi*, but there was a tremendous fund of knowledge and experience, more than any regular Naval ship could ever hope to boast. The crew knew the sea and its dangers, and accepted them. They knew too the very sharp limitations of their ship and accepted these also. And when, in latitude 63° 40′ North, II° 29′ West, at 3 o'clock on the afternoon of Thursday, 23 November, they saw the lean sleek shape of the *Scharnhorst* looming through the ice-cold rain-squalls of the bleak sub-Arctic waters, they knew that this was indeed the end, but they accepted that also.

On the bridge, Captain Edward Coverley Kennedy, called back to the colours after seventeen long years in the unwanted wilderness of civilian life, had seen the danger and recognized its implications even before any of his men. He wrongly identified the ship as the *Deutschland*, but the mistake was one of academic importance only: he rightly identified it as a German pocket battleship or battle-cruiser, 26,000-ton leviathans with 13-inch armour-plate and nine 11-inch and twelve 5.9 guns capable of delivering a 8,000-pound broadside in reply to his own puny 400 – and his light 100-pound shells could never hope to penetrate that massive armour anyway.

Even as she emerged from the rain-squalls the *Scharnhorst*'s big signalling lamp was stuttering out the command to 'Heave-to'. The sensible thing, the wise and politic thing – for which there couldn't possibly have been any reproach – would have been to do as the *Scharnhorst* ordered. But with Kennedy, as with most of the great British naval

captains down the centuries, prudence in the face
of the enemy was a quality that he had never
learned, and certainly never inherited. He knew
he could neither fight nor outrun the *Scharnhorst*,
but there were sheltering icebergs and fogbanks
nearby and, while there remained even one
chance in a thousand he was determined to take
it. He ordered the wheel to be put hard over and
smoke floats to be dropped to cover their with-
drawal.

The *Rawalpindi* was still heeling over on her
turn when the *Scharnhorst* again ordered her to
'Heave-to'. This time the message was reinforced
with an 11-inch shell that crashed into the sea just
ahead, sending a tall, slender column of white-
streaked water towering far into the rain-filled
darkening sky, twice the height of the tip of the
Rawalpindi's main mast. Kennedy acknowledged
the weight of the warning by turning even further
away from the enemy and dropping more smoke
floats.

And then, for a moment, he thought salvation
had come. Far off on the starboard bow, a long
dark ship, white water piled high at its bow,
emerged out of rain-squall, arrowing in towards
the scene. One of their own Northern Patrol cruisers, Kennedy thought jubilantly, almost certainly
the *Newcastle*, and he ordered course altered
towards this haven. Almost at once the bitter
truth struck him, but it was too late now. The new

arrival represented not safety but the certain end of everything: it was the *Gneisenau*, sister ship to the *Scharnhorst*.

Even the one chance in a thousand had gone. There could be no escape now and the two pocket battleships, Kennedy knew, could pound his fragile vessel to death in a matter of minutes. There wouldn't even be a semblance of a fight. Captain Edward Kennedy could have placed scuttling charges, surrendered with honour, and, had he succeeded in reaching Britain again, would almost certainly have been given command of another vessel straight away.

But scuttling charges had never played any part in the Kennedy family's long and honourable two hundred year association with the Royal Navy, and Kennedy was certainly not the man ever to think of such things now even although he, probably above all captains, most certainly owed nothing to a Navy and an Admiralty that had court-martialled him in 1922 on a grotesquely unfair charge and, brilliant officer though he was, had axed him from the service in the following year, calling him back only in their hour of need in 1939. But whatever he thought at the time we can only guess at: all we know is what he said as he watched the two pocket battleships bear down on him: 'We'll just fight them both.' As a death sentence for a great ship and hundreds of men, this must rank as the most laconic ever.

And fought them both he did. Three times the *Scharnhorst* ordered him to abandon ship, and on the third time it had its answer – a salvo that fell just short. At the same time, a salvo from the *Rawalpindi* struck the *Gneisenau* amidships, and almost together the two German battle cruisers replied with heavy, accurate and devastating close-range fire.

The first salvo from the *Scharnhorst* crashed into the *Rawalpindi*'s high superstructure, wrecking the boat-deck and killing almost everyone on the bridge: but Captain Kennedy survived. Almost immediately, another salvo of 11-inch shells, this time from the *Gneisenau*, crashed into the main control room of the *Rawalpindi*, and turned it into a lifeless shambles: all semblance of concerted fire now ceased, but the seven guns – one had already been destroyed – fought on independently.

The fires amidships were already beginning to take hold as yet another salvo sliced through the tissue-thin sides of the liner and exploded deep in its heart. One of these blew up in the engine room, completely destroying the dynamos, and this was the blow that effectively carried into execution Kennedy's sentence of death. With the dynamos gone, the electricity supply was destroyed: and the shell hoists from the magazines were worked by electricity.

Kennedy, still fighting with his wrecked ship, from the twisted wreckage that was all that was left of his bridge, issued instructions that every available member of the crew should assist in manhandling shells up from the magazines and rolling them across the heaving, shell-swept deck towards those guns that still kept firing: there were only five left now.

That exposed deck of the *Rawalpindi*, raked by screaming shrapnel and jagged twisted steel, became a blood-soaked abattoir for those who fought to reach the empty breeches of the waiting guns. Some carriers were killed outright, and their shells rolled from side to side with the movement of the ship, through the ever-growing flames and over deck-plates beginning to glow dull red from the heat of the internal fires. Other men were wounded, but ignored their agony: one incredibly gallant man, both legs smashed, wounded to death, and with a shell clutched in his one sound arm, dragged his way along the deck, groping blindly for the breech of the gun that he could not see, swearing that he would get them yet.

The battle was grotesquely one-sided. Shells still crashed into the dying *Rawalpindi* and the end could not be long delayed. Loose ammunition was falling into the fires and exploding far beneath. The entire ship, excepting only the poop and fo'c'sle, was a leaping, twisting map of flame. One by one the guns fell silent, as the enemy destroyed them, as the crews died beside them and the supply of ammunition, cut off by walls of flame, finally stopped altogether.

As a fighting unit the *Rawalpindi* was finished, beaten into silence and submission, all but dead in the water. But the sixty year-old Captain Kennedy was a man who was literally incapable of conceiving of the idea of defeat. He left his shattered bridge, groped through the blazing ruins of the superstructure and along the deck towards the poop: if he could only drop some smoke floats, he thought, he might still sail the *Rawalpindi* to safety. His ship was holed and sinking, damaged beyond help or repair and visibly dying: his guns were gone, his crew was decimated, but still he fought for survival. Such indomitable courage, such unyielding tenacity of purpose when all reason for purpose has long since vanished lies barely within the realms of comprehension.

Captain Kennedy vanished into the smoke and the flame, and died.

He was not long survived by his ship or by all except a tragic minority of the crew that had so magnificently served both himself and the *Rawalpindi*. Another shell from the *Scharnhorst* brought the coup de grace – a tremendous roar and a column of white flame lancing high into the gathering gloom of the evening as the erupting main magazine blew out through the sides and deck and burning superstructure and almost severed the *Rawalpindi* in two.

The guns of the *Scharnhorst* and *Gneisenau* fell silent: every salvo now could only be so much wasted ammunition. For the handful of men still left alive aboard the *Rawalpindi* nothing could be achieved by remaining where they were but a death swifter and even more certain than that offered by the ice-cold waters slowly climbing up the rent and gaping sides of the sinking ship.

Miraculously, almost, two of the lifeboats had survived the ferocity of the Germans' shells, and those few men – twenty-seven in all – who were able, slid down the falls and pulled desperately away from the blazing *Rawalpindi*: at any moment an explosion might reach out and destroy them, or destroy the ship and pull them after it as it sunk swiftly down to the deep floor of the ocean.

These men, picked up by the German ships, were the only survivors apart from a handful rescued the following morning. Most of the others had been killed by shell-fire, burnt to death or trapped below decks and drowned in the rising waters. Some men who could not reach the lifeboats, jumped into the sea, searching frantically for broken bits of boats, oars, wreckage, anything that would offer even a passing moment's security before the numbing cold struck deep and their hearts just stopped beating. And many there were, scattered here and there over the decks and in passages and compartments below, too desperately wounded either to move or to call out, who just sat or lay waiting quietly for the end, for the blessing of the freezing waters that would bring swift release from their agonies.

Two hundred and forty men went down with the *Rawalpindi*, and, in light of the fanatical courage with which they had served both their ship and their commander, it is perhaps not too far-fetched to think that some of those who were still alive when the waters closed over them at 8 o'clock that evening may have derived no little consolation from the thought that if they had to go down with their ship, they could have asked no greater privilege than to do so in the incomparable company of Captain Edward Kennedy.

The Sinking of the Bismarck

PART ONE

Far south of the Arctic Circle, along the great trade routes of the Atlantic, westerly gales die away to a whisper and then the warm sun shines on the long gentle swells. Far to the north, in the numbing cold of the Barents Sea, stretch away the immense reaches of an almost miraculous calm, the sea milk-white from horizon to unbroken horizon for day after endless day. But between these two vast areas, along the belt of the Arctic Circle itself, lie the most bitter seas in the world: and no part of it more bitter, more hostile to man and the puny ships that carry him across the savagery of its gale-torn waters than that narrow stretch of ocean between Iceland and Greenland that men call the Denmark Strait.

From the far-ranging Vikings of a thousand years ago to the time of the modern Icelandic fishermen, ships have sailed through this narrow passage, but they sailed always at their peril, only when necessity dictated, and they never lingered long, never a moment more than they had to. No man, no ship, has ever waited there from choice, but, at rare intervals, some few men and ships have had to do it from necessity; just seventeen years ago this month, two ships, with the hundreds of men aboard them, were just coming to the end of the longest vigil man has ever kept on these dark and dangerous waters.

The ships' companies of His Majesty's Cruisers *Suffolk* and *Norfolk* were tired, tired to the point of exhaustion. They had kept their vigil far too long. Even one winter's day in the Denmark Strait, with twenty hours of impenetrable darkness, driving snow, a sub-zero wind knifing off Greenland's barren ice-cap and the ship rolling and plunging steeply, sickeningly, incessantly, is a lifetime in itself, a nightmare that has no ending. And the *Norfolk* and the *Suffolk* had been there for months on end, had been there all through the grim winter of 1940 and the spring of 1941, suffering incredible hardships of cold and discomfort, always watching, always waiting. The strain of watching never ceased, the tension of waiting never ended.

But now summer, or what passes there for summer, had come to the Denmark Strait, and the struggle merely to exist was no longer an all-exclusive preoccupation. True, the cold still struck deep through the layered Arctic clothing, the pack-ice stretching out from the shores of Greenland was only a mile or two away and the rolling fog banks to the east, off the Icelandic coast, no further distant, but at least the sea was calm, the snow held off and the darkness of the long winter night was gone. Halcyon conditions, almost, compared to those they had so recently known: even so, the strain was now infinitely greater than anything that had ever gone before, the tension bow-tautened almost to breaking point.

At that moment, just after 7 o'clock on the evening of 23 May, 1941, the strain, the tension bore most heavily on one man and one man alone – Captain R. M. Ellis, on the bridge of his cruiser *Suffolk*. He had been there, on his bridge, for two days now without a break, he might be there as long again, even longer, but it was impossible that he relax his unceasing vigilance, even for a moment. Too much depended on him. He was not the senior officer in the area: Rear-Admiral Wake-Walker was in his flagship, the *Norfolk*, but the *Norfolk*, though not far away, was safely hidden in the swirling fog. The ultimate responsibility was that of Captain Ellis, and it was a crushing responsibility. He could fail in what he had to do, he could all too easily fail through no fault of his own, but the disastrous consequences of any such failure were not for contemplation. Britain had already suffered and lost too much: one more defeat, one more blunder and the war could well be lost.

The war was in its twentieth month then, and Britain was alone and fighting for its life. Twenty dark, gloomy and tragic months, a gloom only momentarily lifted by the shining courage of the young pilots who had destroyed the Luftwaffe in the Battle of Britain, but now the road ahead was more dark, more hopeless than ever before, and no light at the end of it.

The Wehrmacht's panzer divisions were waiting, the threat of invasion still a Damoclean sword. We had just been driven ignominiously out of Greece. In that very week, Goering's Eleventh Air Corps, whom Churchill called the flame of the German Army, had launched a ruthless and overwhelming attack on our forces in Crete, and the end was only a matter of brief time. Six million tons of shipping had been lost at sea, 650,000 tons in that April alone, the blackest month of the war, and May might prove even more terrible still, for at the moment when Captain Ellis was patrolling north-east and south-west through that narrow lane of clear water between the Greenland ice and the Icelandic fogs, there were no fewer than ten major freight convoys and one large and vital troop convoy, far scattered and for the most part only thinly protected, sailing over the face of the broad Atlantic.

And what part, people were asking bitterly, was Britain's mighty Home Fleet playing in all this. Our first line of defence, our last hope in the darkest hour, why wasn't it throwing all its great weight into these life and death battles? Why wasn't it patrolling the North Sea and the English Channel (where the Stukas and the Heinkels could have destroyed it between dawn and sunset on any given day) ready to smash any cross-Channel invasion? Why hadn't it helped in the evacuation of Greece? Why wasn't it north of Crete, breaking up the seaborne reinforcements without whom Goering's paratroopers could not hope to complete their conquests? Why wasn't it at sea, bringing its great guns to bear for the protection of these threatened convoys in the submarine infested waters to the west? Why was it lying idle, power-less and useless, in its retreat in Scapa Flow? Why, why, why?

The *Bismarck* was the reason why: an overpow-ering reason why.

Laid down in 1936, launched from the Blohm and Voss shipyards in Hamburg on 14 February, 1939, in the presence of no less a person than the Chancellor of the Third Reich, Adolf Hitler him-self, the *Bismarck* was something to haunt the dreams – or nightmares – of foreign navies the world over. Hitler had a genius for exaggeration, but there was no hint of exaggeration in what he said to its crew when he visited the battleship again in early May, 1941, only the simple truth. 'The *Bismarck*,' he told them, 'is the pride of the German Navy.'

She was indeed. She would have been the pride of any navy in the world. Built in cynical disregard of the 35,000 tons treaty limitations, with an actual tonnage somewhere in the region of 50,000, she was unquestionably the most powerful battleship afloat. She was fast, her speed of over 30 knots a match for any British capital ship: she had an immense beam – far greater than that of any British ship – which provided a magnificently stable firing platform for her eight 15-inch and twelve 6-inch guns – and the German gunnery, far superior to ours, was legendarily accurate under any conditions: and with her heavy armour-plating, double and triple hulls and the infinitely complex sub-compartmentation of the hull itself achieving a hitherto impossible degree of watertight integrity, she was widely believed to be virtually unsinkable. She was the trump card in Admiral Raeder's hand – and now the time had come to play that trump.

The *Bismarck* was out. There could no longer be any question about it. First reported by reconnaissance as moving up the Kattegat on 20 May, she had been photographed in the company of a 'Hipper' class cruiser, by a Spitfire pilot, in Grimstad fjord, just south of Bergen, on the early afternoon of the 21st; at 6.00 p.m. the following day, a Maryland bomber from the Hatston naval air base in the Orkneys, skimming low over the water in appalling flying conditions, flew over Grimstad and

Bergen and reported that the *Bismarck* was no longer there.

The *Bismarck* was out, and there could be no mistake where she was going. There were no Russian convoys to attack – Russia was not yet in the war. She could be racing only for the Atlantic, with the 'Hipper' cruiser – later identified as the *Prinz Eugen* – as her scout, there to savage and destroy our Atlantic convoys, our sole remaining lifelines to the outer world. The 'Hipper' itself, only a 10,000 ton cruiser, had once fallen upon a convoy and sent seven ships to the bottom in less than an hour. What the *Bismarck* could do just did not bear contemplation.

The *Bismarck* had to be stopped, and stopped before she had broken loose into the Atlantic, and it was for this single, precise purpose of stopping her that Admiral Sir John Tovey, Commander-in-Chief of the Home Fleet, had so long and so doggedly held his capital ships based on Scapa. Now was the time for the Home Fleet to justify its existence.

Admiral Tovey, a master tactician who was to handle his ships impeccably during the ensuing four days, was under no illusions as to the grave difficulties confronting him, the tragic consequences were he to guess wrongly. The *Bismarck* could break south-west into the Atlantic anywhere between Scotland and Greenland – a bleak, gale-ridden stretch of fully a thousand miles, with

the all-essential visibility more frequently than
not at the mercy of driving rain, blanketing snow
and great rolling fog banks.

He had to station two squadrons, with two battleships in each squadron – he had no faith in the
ability of any one ship of the line to cope with the
Bismarck – at strategically vital positions some
hundreds of miles apart, the *Hood* and the *Prince of
Wales* south of Iceland, and his own flagship, the
King George V, the *Repulse* and the carrier *Victorious*
west of the Faroes, where, he hoped, they would
be most favourably situated to move in any direction to intercept the *Bismarck*.

But they couldn't move until they knew where
the *Bismarck* was, and Admiral Tovey had had his
watchdogs at sea for a long time now, waiting for
this day to come. Between Iceland and the Faroes
patrolled the cruisers *Birmingham* and *Manchester*,
while up in the Denmark Strait the *Suffolk* and the
Norfolk were coming to the end of a long long wait.

7.20 p.m., 23 May, 1941 and the *Suffolk* was steaming southwest down the narrow channel between
the ice and the fog. If the *Bismarck* came by the
Strait, Captain Ellis guessed, she would almost certainly come through that channel: the ice barred
her way to the west, and, over on the east, no captain was going to take the risk of pushing his battleship through a dense fog at something like thirty
knots, especially a fog that concealed a known

minefield forty miles in length. If she were to come at all, that was the way she would come.

And that was the way she did come. At 7.22 p.m. the excited cry of a sharp-eyed lookout had Captain Ellis and all the watchers on the bridge peering intently through their binoculars out over the starboard quarter, the reported bearing, and one brief glance was enough for Ellis to know that their long exhausting wait was indeed over. Even for men who had never seen it, it was almost impossible to mistake the vast bulk of the *Bismarck* anywhere. (Or so one would have thought – it was to prove tragically otherwise less than twelve hours later.)

Captain Ellis was not disposed to linger. He had done the first – and most important – part of his job, the *Bismarck* and the *Prinz Eugen*, he suddenly realized, were only eight miles away, the *Bismarck*'s guns were lethal up to a range of at least twenty miles, and there had been nothing in his instructions about committing suicide. Quite the reverse – he had been ordered to avoid damage to himself at all costs, to shadow the *Bismarck* and guide the battleships of the Home Fleet into her path. Even as the *Suffolk*'s radio room started stuttering out its 'Enemy located' transmissions to Ellis's immediate commander, Rear-Admiral Wake-Walker in the *Norfolk* and to Sir John Tovey in his battleship far to the south, he swung his cruiser heeling far over in a maximum turn to port and raced into the

blanketing safety of the fog that swirled protec-
tively around them only moments after they had
entered it.

Deep in the mist, the *Suffolk* came round,
manoeuvring dangerously in a gap in the mine-
fields, the all-seeing eye of its radar probing
every move of the German battleship as it
steamed at high speed down through the
Denmark Strait. Then, once it was safely past,
both the *Suffolk* and the *Norfolk* moved into shadowing positions astern, and there they grimly
hung on all through that long, vile Arctic night of
snow-storms, rain-squalls and scudding mist,
occasionally losing contact but always regaining
it in what was to become a text-book classic in
the extremely difficult task of shadowing an
enemy craft at night. All night long, too, the
radio transmissions continued, sending out the
constantly changing details of the enemy's position, course and speed.

Three hundred miles to the south, Vice-Admiral
L. E. Holland's squadron, consisting of HMS *Hood*,
HMS *Prince of Wales* and six destroyers, were
already steaming west-northwest at high speed on
an interception course. The excitement, the anticipation aboard these ships was intense. For them,
too, it was the end of a long wait. There was little
doubt in anybody's mind that battle was now
inevitable, even less doubt that the battle could
have only one ending, that the *Bismarck*, despite

her great power and fearsome reputation, had only hours to live.

With her ten 14-inch guns to the *Bismarck*'s eight 15-inch the *Prince of Wales* herself, our newest battleship, was, on paper at least, an even match for the *Bismarck*. (Only her commander, Captain Leach, and a handful of his senior officers were aware that she was far too new, her crew only semi-trained, her 14-inch turrets, as new and untried as the crew itself, so defective, temperamental and liable to mechanical breakdown that the builders' foremen were still aboard working in the turrets, desperately trying to repair the more outstanding defects as the battleship steamed towards the *Bismarck*.)

But no one, not even the most loyal member of her crew, was staking his faith on the *Prince of Wales*. And, indeed, why should he, when only a few cable lengths away he could see the massive bows of the 45,000-ton *Hood* thrusting the puny waves contemptuously aside as she raced towards the enemy. When the *Hood* was with you, nothing could ever go wrong. Every man in the Royal Navy knew that.

And not only in the Navy. It is seventeen years now since the *Hood* died but none of the millions alive today who had grown up before the Second World War can forget, and will probably never forget, the almost unbelievable hold the *Hood* had taken on the imaginations and hearts of the British public. She was the best known, best loved ship in all our long naval history, a household name to countless people for whom *Revenge* and *Victory* were only words. The biggest, most powerful ship of the line in the inter-war years, she stood for all that was permanent, a synonym for all that was invincible, held in awe, even in veneration. For millions of people she *was* the Royal Navy, a legend in her own lifetime . . . But a legend grows old.

And now, with the long night's high-speed steaming over, the dawn in the sky and the *Bismarck* looming up over the horizon, the legend was about to end forever.

Safely out of range, but with a grandstand view of the coming action, the men of the *Norfolk* and the *Suffolk* watched the *Hood* and the *Prince of Wales*, acting as one under the command of Vice-Admiral Holland, bear down on the *Bismarck* and the *Prinz Eugen. But* even at that distance it was obvious that the two British ships were too close together, that Captain Leach of the *Prince of Wales* was being compelled to do exactly as the *Hood* did instead of being allowed to fight his own ship independently and to the best advantage, and, more incredibly still, that the closing course, their line of approach to the enemy, was all that a line of approach should not be. They were steering for the enemy at an angle broad enough to present the Germans with a splendid target but, at the same time, just acute enough to prevent their rear turrets from being brought into action, with the result that the *Bismarck* and *Prinz Eugen* were able to bring their full broadsides to bear against only half of the possible total of the British guns.

Even worse was to follow. The *Hood* was the first to open fire, at 5.52 a.m., and, for reasons that will never be clearly known, she made the fatal error of concentrating her fire on the *Prinz Eugen*, and did so throughout the battle. The mistake in identification was bad enough, but no worse than the standard of her gunnery: the *Prinz Eugen* emerged from the action unscathed.

The *Bismarck* and *Prinz Eugen*, consequently, were free to bring their entire armament to bear on the *Hood*, who, because of her approach angle, could only reply with her two fore turrets. True, the *Prince of Wales* had now opened up also, but the blunt and bitter truth is that it didn't matter very much anyway: her first salvo was more than half a mile wide of the target, the second not much better, and the third also missed. So did the fourth. And the fifth.

The Germans did not miss. The concentrated heaviness of their fire was matched only by its devastating accuracy. Both were on target – the *Hood* – almost at once, the *Prinz Eugen*'s 8-inch shells starting a fire by the *Hood*'s mainmast within the first minute. The *Bismarck*, too, was hitting now, the huge 15-inch projectiles, each one a screaming ton of armour-piercing steel and high explosive, smashing into the reeling *Hood* and exploding deep in her heart. How often the *Hood* was hit, and where she was hit we will never know, nor does it matter.

All that matters, all that we do know, is what was seen by the survivors of that battle at exactly six o'clock that morning, as the fifth salvo from the *Bismarck* straddled the *Hood*. A stabbing column of flame, white and orange and blindingly incandescent, lanced a thousand feet vertically upwards into the grey morning sky as the tremendous detonation of her exploding magazines almost literally blew the *Hood* out of existence. When the last echoes of the great explosion had rolled away to lose themselves beyond the horizon and the smoke drifted slowly over the sea, the shattered remnants of the *Hood* had vanished as completely as if the great ship herself had never existed.

So, in the twenty-first year of her life, the *Hood* died. This, the first naval engagement of her long life, had lasted exactly eight minutes, and when she went down she took 1,500 officers and men with her. There were three survivors.

PART TWO

The destruction of the *Hood*, the invincible, impregnable *Hood*, came as a tremendous shock both to the Navy and the country at large. It was incredible, it was impossible that this had happened – and the impossible had to be explained away, both verbally and in print, with all speed.

As details of the action were at that time lacking, no mention was made of the *Hood*'s suicidal angle of approach to the enemy, the fatal mistake in identification that led to her firing on the *Prinz Eugen* instead of the *Bismarck*, or of the fact that the standard of her gunnery was so poor that she failed to register even one hit throughout the entire engagement. Perhaps it was as well that these things were not known at the time.

The reasons that *were* advanced at the time – and the source of inspiration of these reasons is not far to seek – were that the *Hood*, of course, had been no battleship but only a lightly-protected battle cruiser, and, even so, that the 15-inch shell that had found her magazine had been one chance in a million. These explanations were utter nonsense.

True, the *Hood* was technically classed as a battle cruiser, but it was just that, a technicality and no more: the fact is that with her 12-inch iron and steel sheathing extending over 560 feet on either side and with her total weight of protective metal reaching a fantastic 14,000 tons, she was one of the most heavily armoured ships in the world. As for the one chance in a million shell, senior naval architects had been pointing out for twenty years that the *Hood*'s magazines were wide open to

shells approaching from a certain angle, a danger
that could easily have been obviated by extra
armour plating. The *Hood*'s design was defective,
badly defective, and the Admiralty was well aware
of this.

No such thoughts as these, it is safe to assume,
was in the mind of Captain Leach of the *Prince of
Wales* as the smoke and the dust of the awesome
explosion cleared away and the *Hood* was seen to
be gone. The *Prince of Wales* was fighting for her
life now, and her captain knew it. Both the
Bismarck and the *Prinz Eugen* had swung their guns
on him as soon as the *Hood* had blown up and
already the deadly accuracy of their heavy and
concentrated fire was beginning to have its effect.
Captain Leach summed up the situation, made his
assessments and didn't hesitate. He ordered the
wheel to be put hard over, broke off the engagement and retired under a heavy smokescreen.

'The ship that ran away'. That was what the
Prince of Wales was called then, the coward battleship that turned and fled: it is an open secret that
ship, officers and men, during the remainder of
the *Prince of Wales*'s short life, were henceforward
treated with aversion and cold contempt by the
rest of the Navy and this opprobium ended only
with the death of the ship and the gallant Captain
Leach a bare seven months later under a savage
Japanese aerial attack off the coast of Malaya. The
opprobrium was more than unjust – it was

grotesquely and bitterly unfair. Once again, the Admiralty must shoulder much of the blame.

In fairness, it was completely unintentional on their part. The trouble arose from their official communiqué on the action, which was no better and no worse than the typical wartime communiqué, in that it tended to exaggerate the damage sustained by the enemy while minimizing our own.

Two statements in the communiqué caused the grievous misunderstanding: 'The *Bismarck* was at one time seen to be on fire' and 'The *Prince of Wales* sustained slight damage'. Why in all the world then, people asked, hadn't the ship which had received only slight damage closed with the one on fire and destroyed it. What possible excuse for running away?

Excuse enough. The fire on the *Bismarck*, while demonstrable testimony to the occasional liveliness of official imaginations, had, in actual fact, consisted of no more than soot shaken loose from her funnel. As for the *Prince of Wales*'s 'slight damage', she had been struck by no fewer than three 8-inch shells and four of the *Bismarck*'s great 15-inch shells, one of which had completely wrecked the bridge, killing everyone there except Leach and his chief yeoman of signals. Furthermore, one of the *Prince of Wales*'s big guns was completely out of action, repeated breakdowns in the others led to their firing intermittently or not at all and the jamming of 'Y' turret shell ring had put the four big guns of that turret – half of Captain Leach's effective armament – out of commission. The *Prince of Wales*, far from being slightly damaged, was badly crippled: to close with her powerful enemy, to expose herself any longer to the murderous accuracy of these broadsides would have been no mere act of folly but quick and certain suicide.

The *Bismarck* made no attempt to pursue and engage her enemy. With the *Hood* destroyed and the *Prince of Wales* badly hurt and driven off in ignominious defeat, she had already achieved success beyond her wildest dreams. A magnificent victory, a tremendous boost to the prestige of the German Navy and, in Goebbels' hands, a new-forged propaganda weapon of incalculable power – why risk throwing it all away by exposing herself to a lucky salvo that might destroy her turrets or bridge or fire control directors – or might even sink her? Besides, her primary purpose in breaking into the Atlantic was not to engage the Home Fleet – that was the last thing Admiral Lutjens wanted – but to annihilate our convoys.

The rejoicing aboard the *Bismarck* was intense, but no more so than the jubilation in the chancellory of Berlin, where news of this resounding triumph had been flashed as soon as the *Bismarck* had broken off the action.

Within an hour the news would be in the hands of every newspaper and radio station in the coun-

try. By the afternoon every person in Germany –
and by the evening every country in Europe –
would know of the crushing defeat suffered by the
Royal Navy. An overjoyed Hitler sent his own and
the nation's congratulations and admiration to the
officers and men of the *Bismarck*, and personally
announced, amongst numerous other decorations,
the immediate award of the Knight's Insignia of the
Iron Cross to the *Bismarck*'s first gunnery officer.

Only one man held aloof, only one man
remained untouched by the exultation, the exhila-
ration of the victory – the man, one would have
thought, who had the greatest cause of all to
rejoice, Captain Lindemann, commanding officer
of the *Bismarck*. Lindemann was unhappy and
more than a little afraid – and no man had ever
called Lindemann's courage into question. A gallant and very experienced sailor, reckoned about
the best and the most skilful in the German Navy –
and he had to be, to have command of the finest
ship in the German Navy – he was filled with foreboding, a dark certainty of ultimate defeat.

Although his ship had suffered no damage
either to her guns or engines and was still the complete fighting machine, a shell, crashing through
the heavy armour, and exploding in her fuel tanks
had perceptibly reduced her speed and he feared
he might not have sufficient fuel left for sustained
high-speed steaming and manoeuvring – and
Lindemann realized only too clearly that he would

require all the speed and every pound of thrust the *Bismarck*'s big turbines were capable of developing. He knew the British, he knew the tremendous regard and affection in which they had held the *Hood*, and he knew too that, far from being intimidated by the appalling manner of her death, they would have been goaded into a savage fury for revenge and would not rest until they had hunted them down and destroyed them.

These fears he tried to communicate to his senior officer, Admiral Lutjens, and suggested that they return immediately to Bergen, for repairs. Admiral Lutjens, for reasons which we will never know – possibly the elation of their great success had temporarily blurred his judgment and dreams of glory are notoriously treacherous counsellors – overruled his captain. They would go on as originally planned. So the *Bismarck* turned south-west and pushed on deep down into the Atlantic.

The Navy followed her. All afternoon and evening the *Norfolk*, *Suffolk* and *Prince of Wales* shadowed both German ships, sending out constant radio transmissions to Admiral Tovey, who swung his squadron on to a new interception course.

The *Bismarck* knew she was being followed, but seemed to be undisturbed by this. Only once, briefly, did she show her teeth. About 6.30 in the evening, she turned on her tracks in a fog bank and opened fired on the *Suffolk*, but broke off the engagement almost at once, when the *Prince of*

Wales joined in. (It was not realized at the time that this was merely a diversion to let the *Prinz Eugen* break away to a German oiler, where she refuelled and made her way safely to Brest.)

The *Bismarck* now turned to the west and the British shadowers followed, Admiral Tovey's squadron still pursuing. But Tovey's *King George V*, *Repulse* and *Victorious* were now only three out of many ships converging on the German capital ship.

The battleship *Revenge* was ordered out from Halifax, Nova Scotia. Vice-Admiral Somerville's Force H – the battle cruiser *Renown*, the now legendary *Ark Royal* and the cruiser *Sheffield* – were ordered up from Gibraltar. The battleship *Ramillies*, then with a mid-Atlantic convoy, the cruiser *Edinburgh*, down near the Azores and the cruiser *London*, with a convoy off the Spanish coast, were all ordered to intercept. Last, but most important of all, the battleship *Rodney* was pulled off a States-bound convoy. The *Rodney* herself was going to Boston for an urgent and long overdue refit, as her engines and boiler-rooms were in a sorely dilapidated state: but the *Rodney*'s great 16-inch guns, and the magnificently Nelsonian capacity of her commander, Captain Dalrymple-Hamilton, to turn a blind eye to what he considered well-meant but erring signals from the Admiralty were to prove more than counter-balance for the parlous state of her engines. The greatest hunt in naval history was on.

Late that evening – just before midnight – Swordfish torpedo bombers from the *Victorious*, nine in all and led by Lieutenant-Commander Esmonde – who was later to lose his life but win a posthumous Victoria Cross for his attack on the *Gneisenau* and *Scharnhorst* – launched an attack against the *Bismarck* in an attempt to slow her. But only one torpedo struck home, exploding harmlessly against the *Bismarck*'s massive armour plating.

Or so the official Admiralty communiqué claimed. For once, however, the claim was an underestimate. Baron von Mullenheim Rechberg (today the German consul in Kingston, Jamaica) but then the lieutenant-commander in charge of the *Bismarck*'s after turret – and the ship's senior surviving officer – said recently, when questioned on this point, that the *Bismarck* had been torpedoed three times by aircraft from the *Victorious*. Two of the torpedoes had little effect, but the third, exploding under the bows, caused severe damage and slowed up the *Bismarck* still more.

And then, at three o'clock on the morning of the 25th, that which both the Admiralty and Sir John Tovey had feared above all else happened – the shadowing ships, zig-zagging through submarine infested waters, made their first and only mistake, broke contact and completely failed to regain it. The *Bismarck* was lost, and no one knew where she was or, worse still, where she was heading.

* * *

Later on that same morning, Admiral Lutjens addressed the crew of the *Bismarck*. The optimistic confidence with which, only twenty-four hours previously, he had scoffed at Captain Lindemann's suggestion that they return to Bergen, had vanished completely. He was now a tired and anxious man, a man who realized all too clearly the enormity of his blunder. Incredibly, it seems that he was unaware that they had shaken off their pursuers – it was thought that they were still being shadowed by radar – and when Lutjens spoke the first overtones of desperation were all too clear in his voice.

The British, he said, knew where they were and it was only a matter of time before their big ships closed in, and in overwhelming force. They knew what the outcome must be. They must fight to the death for the Fuehrer, every last man of them, and, if needs be, the *Bismarck* herself would be scuttled. It is not difficult to imagine what effect this brief speech must have had on the morale of the *Bismarck*'s crew.

Why had Lutjens been so sure that capital ships of the Royal Navy were bearing down on them? In the first place, wrongly believing that he was still being trailed by the *Norfolk* and *Suffolk*, he naturally assumed that they were guiding the British battleships to the scene. Secondly, the *Bismarck* had just been in wireless contact with the German Admiralty – who, says von Mullenheim, were unaware of the true position – and had just received from them, doubtless on the basis of reports from Doenitz's U-boats, information about the whereabouts of her hunters which was not only misleading in itself but made doubly so by errors in transmission. British battleships were reported to be in the close vicinity and, acting on this false information, Lutjens ordered alterations in course which lost the *Bismarck* those few irreplaceable hours that were to make all the difference between life and death.

The *Bismarck*'s radio transmissions were picked up by listening posts in Britain, and the bearings taken. The Admiralty's incredulity that the *Bismarck* should thus suicidally break radio silence and betray its position – they didn't know, of course, that the *Bismarck* still thought she was being shadowed – was equalled only by their immense relief and the alacrity with which they sent these bearings to their Commander-in-Chief, Admiral Tovey.

By an ironic and amazing coincidence – and it happened almost exactly at the same time – just as Lutjens aboard the *Bismarck* had received a completely misleading report on the position of the enemy, so did Tovey on the *King George V.* In Tovey's case, however, the bearings had been correctly transmitted but were wrongly worked out on the plot of the battleship. The result, however, was the same. Both admirals were misled, and misled at a vital moment.

The calculations made on the *King George V* showed that the *Bismarck* was north, instead of, as expected, south of her last reported position. This could mean only one thing – she was headed for Norway and home, instead of Brest, as everyone had thought. There wasn't a moment to lose – even now it might be too late. Tovey at once ordered his far-scattered fleet to turn in their tracks and make for the North Sea.

This every ship did – with the major exception of the *Rodney*. Captain Dalrymple-Hamilton on the *Rodney* doubted that the *Bismarck was*, in fact, making for the North Sea and as he was then sitting nicely astride her escape route to Brest he decided to remain there. Some time later the Admiralty, too, sent him a signal to the same effect, but Dalrymple-Hamilton ignored it, backed his own judgment and stayed where he was.

Later in the afternoon, in an atmosphere of increasingly mounting tension and almost despairing anxiety, further *Bismarck* position reports came in to Tovey that made it clear that the previous estimated *Bismarck* positions had been wrong and that she was indeed heading for Brest. Tovey was deeply worried, for the Admiralty, he knew, had the same information and yet were acquiescing in the Home Fleet's search to the north-east. It is now obvious that some powerful person in the

Admiralty – we shall probably never know who it was as their Lordships can hardly be accused of garrulity as far as the admission and explanation of their mistakes are concerned – was going in the face of all the evidence and backing his wildly wrong hunches.

Admiral Tovey backed his own hunch, decided he could not wait for the Admiralty to make up its mind and turned his fleet for Brest. Or, rather, such as was left of his fleet, for, apart from his own ship, the *Norfolk*, the *Rodney*, the *Dorsetshire* coming up from the south, and the *Renown*, *Ark Royal* and *Sheffield* of Force H, all the others were one by one being forced to retire from the chase by reason of the Admiralty's non-existent fuelling arrangements.

The *Bismarck*, too, was now short of fuel – desperately short. Through some almost unbelievable oversight or carelessness she had left home 2,000 tons of fuel short, and when the *Prince of Wales* shell, during the action with the *Hood*, had smashed into her bunkers, many hundreds of tons more had been lost, either directly to the sea or by salt water contamination. She had hardly enough oil left to reach Brest, even at an economical steaming speed – at a moment when she needed every knot she possessed.

The crew knew this, as crews always get to know these things, and to counteract the breaking morale and steadily mounting despair reports were circulated that an oil tanker was already en route to refuel them, and that, before long, the seas around them would be alive with their own U-boats and the skies black with the bombers of the Luftwaffe, to escort them safely into harbour.

But the oil tanker never came. Neither did the U-boats nor the Luftwaffe. What came instead, after thirty-one hours of increasingly frantic searching by British planes and ships, was a long range Catalina of the Coastal Command. At 10.30 on the morning of 26 May, the long wait was over and the *Bismarck* found again, her last hope gone. She was then about 550 miles west of Land's End, and heading for Brest.

An illuminating comment on the state of the morale at that moment aboard the German battleship is provided by Baron Mullenheim, who says that the *Bismarck* had all prepared for instant use a dummy funnel and set of Naval code recognition signals. But, so frustrated and self-defeated – von Mullenheim's own words – were the crew that neither of these were used at the very moment when it might have been the saving of the *Bismarck*.

Sir John Tovey's relief, just as he was convinced that the enemy had finally escaped him, must have been immense – but it was shortlived. His ship and the *Rodney*, with whom he was now in contact, were, he soon realized, much too far behind the enemy to cut him off before he reached Brest. Neither the *Norfolk*, the *Dorsetshire* nor the five destroyers under the command of Captain Vian on the *Cossack*, recently pulled off a southbound convoy, could even hope to stop the *Bismarck* – they would have been blown out of the water before they had even begun to get within gun or torpedo range. The last remaining hope of stopping the *Bismarck* lay with the aircraft of the *Ark Royal*, approaching rapidly from the south.

Accordingly, at 3 p.m. in the afternoon of the 26th, torpedo carrying Swordfish took off in what was regarded at the time as a last desperate effort to stop the *Bismarck*. In the words of the official communiqué, 'the attack proved unsuccessful'. This was hardly surprising in view of two facts that were not mentioned in the Admiralty's communiqué – many of the torpedoes, fitted with experimental magnetic warheads, exploded on contact with the water, which was just as well as, by what might have been a tragic mistake in identification, the attack was directed not against the *Bismarck* but their own escorting destroyer, the *Sheffield*.

Admiral Tovey was now in despair. There was, he felt, no stopping the *Bismarck* now. Both he and the *Rodney*, by that time desperately short of fuel, would have to turn for home in only a matter of hours and allow the *Bismarck* to continue unmolested to Brest. It would have been the cruellest blow of his long and illustrious career.

The blow never fell. Sir John Tovey, and, indeed, the entire Royal Navy, were saved from this bitterest of defeats by a handful of young Fleet Air Arm pilots on the *Ark Royal*, who were desperately determined to redeem their ignominious blunder of that afternoon.

And redeem it they did. In almost a full gale, in rain squalls and poor visibility, they somehow, miraculously, took off from the treacherously wet, plunging, rolling flight deck of the *Ark Royal*, sought out the *Bismarck* in appalling flying weather and pressed home their attack, in face of intense anti-aircraft fire, with splendid gallantry. Only two torpedoes struck home – von Mullenheim says three, but the number is unimportant. Only the last torpedo counted, and that one, exploding far aft on the starboard quarter, buckled and jammed the rudders of the great battleship. The *Bismarck* circled twice, then came to a stop, unmanageable and dead in the water, 400 miles due west of Brest. The long chase was over and the *Bismarck* was at bay.

PART THREE

Thus, with the crippling of her steering gear by the torpedo bombers of *Ark Royal*, began the agonizing last night of the brief life of the *Bismarck*.

The greatest battleship in the world was about to go to her death, and it was almost as if nature knew that nothing could now stay her end, for the weather that night was in dark and bitter harmony with the moods, the thoughts, the bleak and sombre despair of the hundreds of exhausted men who still kept watch aboard the *Bismarck*.

The wind blew hard, the cold, driving rain lashed pitilessly across their faces, the waves ran high and rough and confused and the darkness was as absolute as darkness ever becomes at sea: there was no moon that night, and even the stars were hidden by the scudding rain-clouds.

Dead in the water, engines stopped, the *Bismarck* lay in the troughs between the great Atlantic combers rolling heavily, continuously, while the engine room crews worked frantically to free the jammed rudders. Their lives, the life of every man in the ship, depended on the success or failure of their efforts: Brest and safety were only twelve hours' steaming away, even six hours would have taken them under the protective umbrella of their own Luftwaffe, and there no British battleship would dare venture. But with steering control lost, they were helpless.

One rudder was freed and centred, and there it jammed, but even that was a major step forward: if the other could be freed, or even centred so as to eliminate its drag, there would still be hope, for the battleship could be steered by varying the relative speeds of the two great propellor shafts to overcome the contending forces of wind, wave and tide. But the rudder, buckled and twisted by the impact of the torpedo explosion, remained far over at its acute angle, immovably jammed.

The situation was desperate. Time was running out, and the engineers, haggard, exhausted men who had almost forgotten what sleep was, were now all but incapable of any effort at all, mental or physical: with the interminable plunging of the wildly rolling ship and the fumes of diesel oil seeping back from ruptured fuel tanks even the most experienced sailors among them were almost continually sick, many of them violently so.

It was announced that the man who succeeded in freeing the rudders would be awarded the Knight's Insignia of the Iron Cross – the highest award Germany can bestow. But there is no place for dreams of glory in the utter wretchedness of a seasick man, and even had a diver gone over the side into that black and gale-wracked sea he could have achieved nothing except his own death, and that in a matter of moments as the great ship, wallowing wickedly in the troughs, crushed the life out of him.

The engineer commander approached Captain Lindemann with a counsel of desperation – they should try to blow the rudder off with high explosive. Lindemann, who had had no sleep for six days and six nights replied with the massive indifference of one who has taken far too much and for whom nothing now remains, 'You may do

what you like. I have finished with the *Bismarck*.'
These, surely, are the most tragic words that have
ever been uttered by the commander of a naval
vessel, but it is impossible to blame Captain
Lindemann: in his hopelessness, in his black
despair and utter exhaustion, he was no longer in
contact with reality.

The order was given – it may have been by
Admiral Lutjens himself – to get under way, and
slowly the *Bismarck* gathered speed until she was
doing almost ten knots. With no steering control
left, she yawed wildly from side to side, but her
general course was north – towards the coast of
England. This was the last thing Lutjens wanted,
but there was no help for it: with the constant lifeless rolling in the great troughs, the turret crews
had become so seasick that they were unable to
fight their guns, and the ship itself had become a
most unstable firing platform. More important
still, a ship lying stopped in the water was a sitting
target for any torpedo attacks that might be deliv-
ered in the darkness of the night.

And, inevitably, the torpedo attacks came. All
night long the *Bismarck* was harassed by a group of
British destroyers, who, with their vastly superior
speed and manoeuvrability, circled it like a pack of
hounds waiting to bring down and finish off a
wounded stag. But the *Bismarck*, as the destroyers
found, was not to be finished off so easily. Time
and again, as a hound darts in to nip the stag, a

destroyer raced in and loosed off its torpedoes, but soon discovered that this was an unprofitable and highly dangerous proceeding. Somehow, somewhere, the *Bismarck*'s gun crews – and they were, after all, the pick of the German Navy – had found their last reserves of spirit and energy and drove off the British destroyers with heavy and extremely accurate radar-controlled fire from their 15-inch turrets.

During the running and intermittent battle, in the intervals between the crash of the gunfire and the momentary glaring illumination of the ship and sea around as the white and orange flames streaked from the mouths of the big barrels, a German naval officer, intent on boosting the morale of his men, kept up a commentary of the fight over the Tannoy system. 'One British destroyer hit . . . One hit and on fire . . . Ship blowing up and sinking . . .'

(In point of fact, none of Captain Vian's destroyers were hit, far less sunk, during the night. It is as well to remember, however, that all the inventiveness was not on the German side. The British destroyers claimed, a claim that was backed by the official Admiralty communiqué, that the *Bismarck* had been torpedoed several times during the night: the truth is that the *Bismarck* wasn't hit even once by a torpedo.)

Early on in the night, the Fuehrer himself sent a personal message to the *Bismarck*: 'Our thoughts are with our victorious comrades' to which he

received a reply, 'Ship completely unmanoeu-
vrable. Will fight to the last shell.'

It is difficult to imagine which of the two messages had the more dismaying effect. Probably the
latter. For doomed men to be addressed as 'victorious comrades' is irony enough, but for Hitler to
learn that all hope had been abandoned for the
magnificent ship he had visited only a week or
two previously and called the pride of the German
Navy must have been a shattering blow.

As Lutjens said, the ship was completely un-
manoeuvrable. The long dark night wore on, and
in spite of every effort it proved impossible to
bring the *Bismarck* round on a course for Brest. For
her own safety she had to keep moving, and with
the set of the wind and the sea, there was only
one way she could move – north.

Dawn was coming up now, a bleak, cheerless
dawn with driving rain clouds and a grey and
stormy sea. There was no longer any hiding from
the crew the course they were steering, and the
despair and the fear lay heavy over the *Bismarck*.
It was almost certainly to counteract this that an
official message was passed round to the men at
their stations – those who still fought off exhaustion and remained awake at their stations – that
squadrons of Stukas had already taken off from
Northern France, and that a tanker, tugs and
escorting destroyers were steaming out to their
aid. There was no word of truth in this. The

Luftwaffe was grounded by the same high wind and low, gale-torn rain clouds as were sweeping across the *Bismarck*, the tugs and tanker were still in Brest harbour and the destroyers never came.

There came instead the two most powerful battleships of the British Home Fleet, the *Rodney* and the *King George V*, beating up out of the west so as to have the *Bismarck* between them and the lightening sky to the east. The men of the *Bismarck* knew that there would be no escape this time, that the promised Stukas and destroyers and U-boats would never come, and that when the British battleships, bent on revenge for the sunken *Hood*, finally turned for home again they would leave an empty sea behind them. The *Bismarck* made ready to die.

Over the guns, by the great engines, in the magazines and fire-control rooms, exhausted men lay or sat by their posts, sunk in drugged uncaring sleep. On the bridge, according to the testimony of one of the few surviving officers, senior officers lay at their stations like dead men, the helmsman was stretched out by the useless wheel, of the Admiral or any member of his staff there was no sign. They had to be shaken and beaten out of the depths of their so desperately needed sleep, awakened to the cruellest, the most bitter dawn they had ever known: and, for all but a handful, it was their last awakening.

Even before they were all roused, closed up at their battle stations and ready to defend themselves, the *Rodney*, no more than four minutes after she had first been sighted, opened up with her great 16-inch guns. For the waiting men on the *Bismarck*, the spectacle of a full-scale broadside from the *Rodney*, with her three massive triple turrets all ranged together on her tremendously long fore-deck and firing simultaneously as they did later in the battle, was an impressive and terrifying sight: but no more terrifying than the express train shriek of the approaching salvo, the flat thunderclaps of sound as the shells exploded on nearby contact with the water, the waterspouts erupting two hundred feet up into the leaden sky.

But this first salvo missed. So, almost immediately afterwards, did the first from the *King George V*. And now the *Bismarck* retaliated and concluding, probably rightly, that the *Rodney* was the more dangerous opponent, directed the first salvo at her. It fell a long way short, but the *Bismarck*'s reputation for gunnery of a quite extraordinary accuracy, a reputation achieved in only four brief days, was solidly founded in fact: almost immediately she started straddling the *Rodney*, which took swift avoiding action.

But still the *Rodney* was firing from every gun that could be brought to bear, and the *King George V*, temporarily ignored by the *Bismarck*, was arrowing in head-on, her six big for'ard 15-inch guns firing time and again, as quickly as they could be reloaded. The *Norfolk*, too, the cruiser that had doggedly followed the *Bismarck* all the way from the far-distant waters of the Denmark Strait, now joined in the fight and shortly afterwards the *Dorsetshire*, who had taken a severe hammering all night long as she had raced north through gale-winds and heavy seas, appeared on the scene. Within fifteen minutes from the beginning of the action, the *Bismarck* was being subjected to heavy and sustained fire from two battleships and two cruisers.

The odds were hopeless. Even for a ship capable of high speed and rapid manoeuvre, and with a fresh and confident crew, the sheer weight of enemy shells would have proved far too much: and the *Bismarck* could now move only at a relative crawl, manoeuvre of any kind was impossible for her and her crew were exhausted, hopeless and utterly demoralized. In retrospect, over the gap of seventeen years, our sympathies tend to lie with the *Bismarck*, a sitting target lying increasingly helpless in the water, being mercilessly battered into extinction. But there was no thought of mercy at the time, only of revenge and destruction, and understandably so: only four days had elapsed since the *Hood* and fifteen hundred men had gone to their deaths – and the Stukas and U-boats might appear on the scene at any moment.

Already, within fifteen minutes of the first shots being fired, there was a marked deterioration in the *Bismarck*'s rate and accuracy of fire. Heavy shells from the two British capital ships were beginning to smash into her, and the concussive impact of the exploding missiles, the clouds of acrid smoke and the bedlam of sound mingling with the crash of their own guns had a devastating and utterly demoralizing effect on the already dazed and exhausted gun crews crouched within their turrets.

Those few officers who still clung stubbornly to the bridge of the *Bismarck* could see that the gunfire from the *King George V* was falling off and becoming increasingly spasmodic (suffering from the same turret troubles as her sister ship the *Prince of Wales*, the *King George V* had, at one time, only two guns out of her ten capable of firing) and ordered every available gun to concentrate on the *Rodney*. But it was too late.

The *Rodney*, close in now, had the range and had it accurately. The big 16-inch shells, each one 2,700 pounds of armour-piercing high explosive, were crashing into the vitals of the shuddering *Bismarck* with steadily increasing frequency. One 16-inch shell struck the fire control tower, blasting it completely over the side, and after that all semblance of concerted firing and defence ceased. Another 16-inch shell silenced both for'ard turrets at once, wrecking 'A' turret and blowing part of 'B' turret back over the bridge, killing most of the officers and men left there. Shells from both battleships were exploding deep in the heart of the *Bismarck*, wrecking the engine rooms, destroying the fuel tanks and adding hundreds of tons of fuel to feed the great fires now raging in the entire mid-section of the ship, the roaring flames clearly visible through the great jagged gaps torn in the ship's side and armour-plating.

'Nightmarish' is the only word to describe the dreadful scenes now taking place aboard that battered, holed and flaming shambles of twisted steel and broken bodies that was all that was left of the *Bismarck* and its crew.

Sixteen-inch shells from the *Rodney*, by this time at a point-blank range of only two miles, were now hitting the *Bismarck* two, four, even six at a time, and groups of fear-maddened men on the upper deck were running blindly backward and forward like crazed animals seeking escape from the twin terrors of these lethal broadsides and the red-hot deck-plates beginning to twist and buckle under their very feet: most of them chose the easy way out, a leap into the shell-torn sea and death by drowning.

In the turrets, sailors abandoned their now useless guns, mutinied and rushed for the turret doors. Some of the commanding officers of the turrets committed suicide, and others turned pistols on their own men, only to be overwhelmed: and then, the men found that the doors were warped and jammed fast, and they went down to the floor of the Atlantic locked in the iron coffin of the turret they had served so well.

Hatches, too, jammed shut all over the *Bismarck*. Two hundred men, imprisoned thus in the canteen, were fighting madly to force their way out, when a shell crashed through the deck and exploded inside, all the concussive blast and murderous storm of flying shrapnel confined to that one narrow space. There were no survivors.

But they were the lucky ones in the manner of their dying – lucky, that is, compared to the ghastly fate of the sailors trapped in magazines. Raging fires surrounded these magazines on nearly every side, and as the metal bulkheads grew steadily hotter until they began to glow dull red, the magazine temperatures soared. That this could have only one end the few damage control men still clinging to their posts knew all too well – and they could never forget the *Hood* blown out of existence when her magazines went up. They had no option but to do what they had to do – flood the magazines and drown their comrades in the swiftly rising waters.

And just as nightmarish as the scenes aboard was the appalling spectacle of the *Bismarck* herself. Weighed down by the thousands of tons of water rushing in through the great gaps torn in her sides, she rolled heavily, sluggishly, in the troughs between the waves, a battered, devastated wreck.

Her mast was gone, her director tower was gone, the funnel had just disappeared. All her boats had been destroyed, the smashed and broken turrets lay over at crazy angles, the barrels pointing down into the sea or up towards an empty sky, and the broken, twisted steel girders and plates of what had once been her superstructure glowed first red, then whitely incandescent as the great fires deep within blazed higher and higher. But still the *Bismarck* did not die.

Beyond all question, she was the toughest and most nearly indestructible ship ever built. She had been hit by the *Prince of Wales*, she had been hit by hundreds of heavy, armour piercing shells from the *King George V*, *Rodney*, *Norfolk* and *Dorsetshire*. She had been torpedoed by aircraft from the *Ark Royal* and from the *Victorious*, and now, in this, her last battle, torpedoed also by the *Rodney* and the *Norfolk*. But still, incredibly, she lived. No ship in naval history had ever taken half the punishment the *Bismarck* had, and survived. It was almost uncanny.

In the end, she was not to die under the guns of the two British battleships that had reduced her to this empty blazing hulk. Perhaps, in their wonder at her incredible toughness, they had come to believe that she could never be sunk by shell-fire. Perhaps it was their dangerous shortage of fuel, or the certainty that U-boats would soon be on the scene, in force: or perhaps they were just sickened by the slaughter. In any event, the *King George V* and the *Rodney*, their mission accomplished, turned for home.

The *Bismarck* never surrendered. Her colours still flew high, were still flying when the *Dorsetshire* closed in on the silent, lifeless ship and torpedoed three times from close range. Almost at once she heeled far over to port, her colours dipping into the water, then turned bottom up and slid beneath the waves, silent except for the furious hissing and bubbling as the waters closed over the red hot steel of the superstructure.

The long chase was over: the *Hood* was avenged.

The Meknes

The English Channel, during the years 1939–1945, was the setting for countless extraordinary and sometimes, during the invasion summer of 1944, frankly incredible spectacles; but it can safely be said that at no time in the war did it present a sight more astonishing, incongruous and utterly improbable than that to be seen on a night in late July in the year 1940, some 60 miles off the Isle of Wight.

This sight was a ship, just an ordinary 6,000-ton cargo and passenger liner, but it was behaving in a most extraordinary fashion. One could have looked at it, then looked again, and still have been excused for flatly disbelieving the plain evidence before one's eyes. During the hours of darkness in the wartime Channel secrecy, stealth, and above all an absolutely enforced blackout, were the essentials without which there was no hope of survival. One careless chink of escaping light, one thoughtlessly struck match or cigarette end glowing in the darkness, and the chances were high that a U-boat's periscope or torpedo boat's bows lined up and locked on the betrayed bearing.

Yet there was light to be seen aboard this ship. *Not just one light, but hundreds of them.* It was as if a section of the Blackpool illuminations had been transferred en bloc to the middle of the Channel. Every blackout scuttle had been removed, and the lights behind the portholes switched on. The lights on deck and on the superstructure blazed. The bridge was floodlit. Powerful projectors lit up the name and nationality marks painted on either side of the hull, while another illuminated the big flag painted on the deck. Finally, two powerful searchlights were trained on the tricolour flag that fluttered high above the stern.

The night was fairly calm, the sky clear, visibility good: the brilliantly illuminated vessel must have been clearly visible over at least 500 square miles of the Channel and over 10 times that area for any plane cruising overhead.

The ship was the *Meknes*, owned by the *Compagnie Générale Transatlantique*, and she had excellent reason for this blatant self-advertisement. Or at least, tragically, so it was imagined at the time.

The *Meknes* was en route from Southampton to Marseilles with 1,180 French naval officers and ratings, mostly reservists who had served aboard a French battle-cruiser until the fall of their country, then transferred to Britain. They had since elected to return to their own country. Marseilles, at that time, was technically a neutral port, and these repatriates were non-combatants: the French Vichy Government, under the aged Marshal Pétain, had just concluded a separate peace with Germany. The French repatriates, therefore, were entitled to be regarded as neutrals, and afforded the protection that international law demands for neutrals. Accordingly, the British Government had informed Vichy of the repatriation, with instructions that the Germans be advised and asked to provide a safe conduct. Precautions would be taken, the British added, to ensure that there would be no mistaking her identity.

And there most certainly was no mistaking her identity, when the *Meknes* left Southampton at 4.30 p.m., cleared the Isle of Wight, and steamed down the Channel at fifteen knots.

All went well for the first few hours, and even the most apprehensive were beginning to relax, becoming increasingly confident that the guarantee of safe conduct was being scrupulously observed, when, at 10.30 p.m., the officer of the watch heard the sound of powerful motor engines closing rapidly. Blinded by the intensity of the *Meknes*'s own lights, he was unable to make out even the silhouette of the approaching boat, but the phosphorescent gleam of the high creaming wake it left behind it and the familiar sound of the engines left him in no doubt at all – it was a German E-boat, out on the prowl. At once he picked up the phone to report to the *Meknes*'s commander, Captain Dulroc, but before he had even begun to speak, the E-boat opened up with its machine guns, raking the super-structure, deck and port side of the ship with heavy and concentrated fire.

Captain Dulroc, ignoring the fire, rushed to the bridge while all around him machine-gun bullets smashed with triphammer thuds against steel bulkheads, and whined off in evil ricochet into the darkness beyond. Dulroc still believed in his guar-antee of safe passage. He was convinced this was an error in identification that could soon be recti-fied. He rang the engine room telegraphs to *stop*, and gave two prolonged blasts on the ship's whis-tle to show that he was no longer under way. The machine-gun fire ceased almost at once, and Dulroc flashed out a 'Who are you?' signal.

The reply came immediately – an even heavier burst of fire directed against the bridge with such venom and accuracy that officers and men had to fling themselves flat on their faces to escape the murderous barrage.

Again there came a brief lull in the firing, and Dulroc swiftly seized the opportunity to send out morse signals in the general direction of their still invisible assailant giving the name, nationality and destination of the *Meknes* over and over again. But the E-boat captain seemed beyond either rea-

son or appeal. He opened fire again, this time not
only with machine guns but with heavier calibre
weapons, probably something in the nature of
two-pounders.

Within seconds every lifeboat but one on the
port side was smashed and made useless. Captain
Dulroc and his officers had no illusions left now.
The earlier bursts of machine-gun fire might have
been the results of misidentification or over-
enthusiasm on the part of a trigger-happy young
torpedo-boat captain. But the destruction of their
port lifeboats had been no accident. They were
clearly visible and sharply etched against the surrounding darkness by the numerous deck-and
floodlights that were still switched on. The E-boat
had deliberately aimed at and destroyed them
with its heavy gun, and the reason for this
destruction was not far to seek.

*It had destroyed their boats so that they could not be
used – and their only use, of course, could be for the saving of survivors. The* Meknes, *Dulroc knew, was going
to be destroyed.*

At 10.55 p.m. the now inevitable torpedo was
fired from almost point-blank range. One of the
survivors, M Macé, says that he was talking to
some friends in his cabin, discussing the machine-
gun attacks, when a terrific explosion burst in the
cabin walls and threw the men, one on top of the
other, in a confused heap in the middle of the cabin
deck. Somebody cried out, rather unnecessarily as

Macé drily observes, 'We have been torpedoed.' They rose dazedly to their feet and burst their way out through the broken splintered door on to the open deck, to find the ship already sinking beneath their feet, going down rapidly by the stern. But it was not that unnaturally canted angle of the ship that attracted Macé's attention at that moment. The torpedo struck opposite number three hold – and there were over 200 men confined in that one narrow space.

Macé still remembers, with what he describes as a horrifying vividness, the screams, the moans, and the pitiful wailing of the trapped, the wounded, the dying and the drowning in that deathtrap far beneath his feet.

For the great majority of men down there death came swiftly. Many had died outright and most of those who survived were too badly hurt to make more than a token attempt to escape the all-engulfing flood of hundreds of tons of water that rushed in through the great hole in the ship's side. At the most, Macé says, a dozen men escaped from number three hold. The situation, he goes on, was almost as dreadful on the fo'c'sle of the ship. He could clearly see it from where he stood, even though the lights had died with the blowing up of the boilers. There had, of course, been no direct damage in the fore part of the ship – only one torpedo had struck the *Meknes*. But there was another and almost equally terrifying and lethal agent at work there. The stern of the *Meknes* was already sinking below the surface of the sea, bringing the bows of the ship high up into the air until the fore-foot was almost clear of the water. As the angle increased, heavy rafts, several of them already par-tially released, broke free from their remaining lashings and slid down and aft along the decks, maiming, crushing and killing against bulkheads, rails and stanchions groups of men so tightly knot-ted that for most of them there could be no escape.

Here the first officer of the *Meknes*, now Captain Philippe Gilbert, takes up the story. The master, he says, realized at once that there was no hope of saving the *Meknes*. He ordered an SOS to be sent out – on the emergency radio, as all electricity supplies had been cut off – and for the boats to be lowered at once. Such lifeboats as were still fit to be launched, Gilbert says, were in the water with quite remarkable speed. Although he himself was in direct over-all charge of the lowering, he claims no credit for this. *The loss of life, he is certain, would have been far greater had it not been for the happy chance that nearly all the repatriate passengers were themselves sailors, and most of them experienced sailors at that.* They did not have to be told what to do. They just did it, and at once.

Never had speed and training served men bet-ter. The *Mekne's* end was as swift as it was spectac-ular: she broke completely beneath the surface of the Channel in less than eight minutes from the moment of impact of the torpedo, but in that time every serviceable life-boat – and almost every available raft – was in the water.

As an aside at this point, Captain Gilbert mentions one of the most remarkable things he has ever seen at sea. As the sinking vessel rolled over on its side, one of the men struggling nearby had an extraordinary experience – and escape. 'As one of the ship's funnels tipped over into the water,' Gilbert recalls, 'this man was sucked into it as by a huge vacuum cleaner. Moments later a violent counter-pressure from the other end of the funnel blew him back into the sea. He was completely black from head to foot.'

The man who is now a pilot in Marseilles was one of the lucky ones. Many of those who escaped safely from the ship did so only to die during the night.

Some of the lifeboats had capsized, one or two to drift away, empty, into the darkness. Another was found to have its buoyancy tanks ripped open by machine guns and foundered soon after launching, throwing its occupants into the sea. For the majority, therefore, rafts and floating pieces of timber – of which there were providentially plenty – were the chief means and hope of salvation. In the two minutes before the foundering of the *Meknes*, hundreds of men had leaped into the sea and swum towards the bobbing rafts, dragging themselves aboard as best they could. *The rafts, Macé says, were soon grossly overloaded. Further, the sea was not nearly so calm as it had appeared from the deck of the* Meknes *only an hour or so previously; and the combination of the overloaded rafts and unsettled sea proved an evil one.*

The rafts sank under the surface of the sea, and soon most of the men found themselves chest deep in the water – and even in July the waters of the English Channel can be bitterly cold. Time and again a wave would sweep over a raft and carry a man away: the more fortunate made their way back again and scrambled aboard – if that word can be used to refer to regaining position on something two feet below the level of the sea. Again and again, Macé says, a false movement, an unconscious shifting of position and weight at the critical moment when the other side of the raft was tilting upwards under the thrust of a passing wave and the entire raft would capsize, throwing everybody into the sea. After this had happened repeatedly, only the strongest men succeeded in regaining the raft. Others sank, exhausted or choked, and were never seen again.

And if the fight for sheer physical survival were not enough, there was a still further danger – the enemy who had so recently sunk them. Survivors claimed that they had been fired at in the water when swimming towards the rafts. Though this was probably true, it is unlikely that much loss of life was caused by it. A swimmer in a darkened sea makes a poor target, and it is significant that neither Macé nor Gilbert, two witnesses whose observations and

accuracy of judgment were of the highest order,
sought to dwell on this. It appears reasonably
certain that, once men had reached rafts or
lifeboats, no further attacks were made on them,
although one survivor, the purser of the *Meknes*,
claims that men on rafts *were* machine-gunned
and killed. So brief and utterly confused was the
entire course of events that the facts are difficult
to arrive at.

All night long almost 1,000 men – and two
women, officers' wives, and a five-year-old boy –
waited for rescue, some in boats, but most of them
just clinging to rafts and floating pieces of wood.

Soon after dawn a plane flew over the area, and
within a very short time – for the coast of England
was only two hours' steaming away – the
Frenchmen in the water were overjoyed to see
four British warships steaming down on them at
high speed.

The rescue work was swift and efficient, and all
the survivors – with the exception of some who
were thought to have made for the French coast
and another couple of lifeboats, with 100 sailors in
them, that had to be searched for and located by a
Blenheim bomber – were back in England in a few
hours.

Newspaper reports of the time speak of the
pathetic spectacle these survivors presented –
most of them only in inadequate scraps of clothing, some in pyjamas, some in underclothes, and

not a few with no clothes at all. They were dressed in whatever came to hand – some even in women's frocks – fed in naval barracks and sent to await the next attempt at repatriation in the chalets of a former holiday camp in the northeast. All, that is, except the 150 officers and men who had to be taken straight to hospital.

It was one of the war's major sea disasters. Almost 300 Frenchmen, none of whom was at that time a combatant, lost their lives that July night. And when it comes to the prime or first cause of the tragedy it is as difficult to discover the precise truth as it is to apportion the blame. There is no question, of course, as to the immediate cause of the sinking. The Germans made rather ridiculous attempts to lay the loss at the door of the First Lord of the Admiralty, Mr A. V. Alexander, on the fantastic ground that he had ordered the sinking of the *Meknes* as a propaganda movement to stir up anti-German feeling in France. In fact the responsibility for the sinking was obvious, as the Germans issued a statement on 25 July saying that one of their torpedo boats had sunk a ship south of Portland – precisely where the *Meknes*, the only ship that had been sunk for some considerable time in that area, had been that night.

The ship they had sunk, the Germans claimed, was an 18,000-ton armed merchant cruiser – an obvious fabrication and attempt to explain away their embarrassment at sinking an unarmed neutral with all lights on. Later, the Germans changed their tactics. If the *Meknes* had been sunk by them, they claimed, it was still the fault of Britain. A broadcast by the official German News Agency stated that Britain had not asked for a safe conduct for this vessel, and had not advised the German authorities of the ship's departure and route.

This, as first sight, was another bare-faced fabrication. Most of the British national newspapers, reporting the disaster, had attacked the perfidy of the Germans who had sunk a ship to which they had given an unconditional guarantee of safe passage. However, on the following day, to the accompaniment of no great beating of drums, there was an official British retraction of the statement that the Germans had given a safe passage guarantee. What had actually happened, it was carefully explained, was that the Vichy Government had been informed of the British intentions and it had been their duty to pass the news to the Germans.

It appeared, in fact, that not only had the Germans not given a safe passage guarantee – it wasn't even certain that they knew anything at all about it.

Here the Vichy Government stepped in. The French Admiralty stated unequivocally that the British Government had failed to inform them of the sailing of the *Meknes*, its route, or even its destination. The effect of this statement in certain circles in this country can well be imagined.

Suggestions then appeared in the British Press – it is a fair indication of the extent to which wartime chauvinism (if not indeed something even more sinister) can affect the judgment of experienced journalists – that the Vichy Government had in fact received all the information, passed on to the Germans the news where a sitting, a defenceless target was to be found, and then officially denied that they had received any information at all from the British.

As a solution, this appears extraordinarily unlikely. Had that been the case, the Germans would not have reacted so clumsily to the accusation of the sinking, and would, indeed, have had their story cut and dried, and, the ship safely sunk, indignantly denied all knowledge of it; and it seems improbable in the extreme that any Frenchman would have willingly and however indirectly been the agent responsible for sending perhaps over 1,000 of his countrymen to their deaths.

There can be little doubt that the prime responsibility for the tragic loss of the Meknes *lies squarely at the door of the British Government.* The official German News Agency said at the time: 'It was the duty of the British Government to inform the French Government of their intention to repatriate French soldiers and to wait for a reply as to whether the dangerous transport through the war zone could be assured of safe convoy.'

Did the British Government in fact so inform the French? An 'authoritative' British source said: 'The French . . . were notified in general terms of our intention to repatriate,' a vague, obscure and weak-kneed attempt at excuse-making that could hardly be bettered.

The French said flatly that they were not informed of the sailing of the Meknes.

What is beyond all dispute – and this is the crux of the matter – no safe conduct or guarantee was given by the Germans. Yet the criminally negligent decision was made to permit the sailing of this unarmed and unescorted vessel into the E-boat and U-boat infested Channel without waiting for a reply from the Germans. It would be interesting indeed to know what British Service or Government department was responsible for this decision. But one can safely assume that the blanket of official anonymity which covers up such a multitude of sins will remain firmly where it is and that none of the parties concerned is going to lift even a tiny corner lest the answers be found to lie uncomfortably close to home.

Besides, in the press of events of a great world war, the death of 300 non-combatants is a small thing, quickly and comfortably forgotten as the first sharp horror of the tragedy fades and finally passes away.

MacHinery and the Cauliflowers

'I find you well, Mr MacHinery?' Ah Wong asked courteously. He pronounced the name as 'Mackinelli' and although ten years in the Far East had accustomed MacHinery to this heathenish mispronunciation of a legendary Scottish clan name that ranked in antiquity with anything the Almanac de Gotha had to offer, nevertheless his proud Celtic soul winced whenever he heard it. Still, he reflected charitably, it was hardly Ah Wong's fault. Some parts of the world were still emerging from the caves, so to speak. Primitive, barbaric – in fact, MacHinery conceded generously to himself, very like the MacHinerys of a few centuries ago when the more pressing business activities of cattle-thieving and hacking opposing clansmen to pieces had left them little time for the more cultural pursuits of life. But twenty intervening generations had had their civilizing effect . . .

MacHinery fingered a beer bottle scar received in a political debate in Glasgow many years previously, and smiled tolerantly.

'I'm weel enough, Mr Wong. Fair to middling, you ken.'

'You do not look it,' Ah Wong said slowly. 'You are pale but you perspire freely. You perspire but you shiver and shake. And your eyes are not the eyes of a well man.' He turned to a wall cabinet and poured amber liquid into a tumbler. 'A well-tried specific from your own homeland, Mr MacHinery.'

'Och, man, it was chust what I was needing.' MacHinery drank deeply, shuddered violently and coughed until the tears rolled down his cheeks. Ah Wong looked at him with suddenly narrowed eyes. Less than a month had elapsed since two sailors had inconsiderately dropped dead after drinking, in one of his emporiums, a bottle of what had purported to be proprietary Scotch and had it not been for the prompt midnight transfer of a couple of barrels of wood alcohol to the go-down of a cherished enemy and the sending to the authorities of a letter signed 'Pro Bono Publico', he might have been in trouble indeed. As it was, any adverse reaction to his Scotch now struck deep at Ah Wong's sensitive soul.

'You do not like my whisky, Mr MacHinery?' he asked slowly.

'Not like it?' MacHinery coughed. 'Hoots, mon, it's perfect, chust perfect.' MacHinery had, in fact, the misfortune to be allergic to any type of whisky but the part of the hard-drinking Clydeside engineer was no more difficult to sustain than the phoney accent that went with it. 'Chust a touch of fever, Mr Wong, that's all.' Experience had long shown him that no one cared whether the fever in question was chickenpox or the Black Plague.

'So.' Ah Wong relaxed a minute fraction, the most he ever permitted himself to relax. 'And you are the new chief engineer of the *Grasshopper*, Mr MacHinery?'

'For ma sins,' MacHinery said bitterly. 'A filthier, rustier, auld bucket of bolts – '

'Beggars cannot be choosers, Mr MacHinery,' Ah Wong said coldly. He waved a piece of paper. 'And you are a beggar. According to this letter of introduction from my good friend Benabi, you'd been in the Djakarta gutters for weeks before he gave you this job. Even your chief engineer's ticket is a forgery – your real one was taken from you.'

'Aye, and a grosser miscarriage of justice – '

'Be quiet,' Ah Wong said contemptuously. 'The *Grasshopper*'s cargo has been unloaded and cleared through customs?'

'Aye. Not thirty minutes ago.' MacHinery shivered again and stirred restlessly in his seat. Sweat poured down his face. Ah Wong affected not to notice.

'Good. You will have been given a private copy of the manifest.' He stretched out his hand. 'Let me see it.'

'Well noo, chust wait a minute,' MacHinery said cunningly. 'You ken who I am. The letter tells you. But I don't ken who *you* are. How do I know you ken one another? You and Benabi, I mean?'

'Fool,' Ah Wong said shortly. 'I, one of the biggest food importers in Malaya? Benabi, of Benabi's Tjitarum's truck farms, the biggest suppliers in Indonesia? Not know each other? Idiot!'

'There's nae call to be personal,' MacHinery said doggedly. 'I hae ma orders, Mr Wong. From Mr Benabi himself. You must match this, he says.' He drew a piece of rice paper from his wallet and showed Ah Wong a curious ink marking, smaller than a thumbnail.

'Of course,' Ah Wong smiled. He twisted a signet ring on his middle finger, pressed it on an ink pad and made an identical mark on the paper. 'The seal of the broken junk. We have the only two such signet rings in the world. Benabi and I – we are brothers.'

'You wouldna think it,' MacHinery said candidly. 'He's a tall, well built, good-looking cove, whereas you –'

'I spoke metaphorically,' Ah Wong said coldly. 'The manifest, Mr MacHinery.'

'Aye.' MacHinery rose, opened the Gladstone bag he'd left in the middle of the floor of Ah Wong's sumptuous apartment, fished out a manifest and handed it over.

'Why the bag?' Ah Wong asked in idle curiosity.

'Why the bag?' MacHinery echoed bitterly. 'The *Grasshopper*'s two nights in Singapore and if you think I'm going to spend them aboard yon bloody flea-ridden, cockroach-infested hellhole, you – '

'Silence!' Ah Wong opened the manifest. 'Ah, yes. Sides of beef, one hundred. Of pork, two hundred. Bananas, onions, beans, peppers, eggplants, butter. Yes, yes, all seems there. Best Bandung cauliflowers, eighty crates. Lettuce, fifty. Yes, all in order.' He broke off, looked thoughtfully at MacHinery and said in Cantonese: 'I am going to kill you, my friend.'

'Whit was that?' MacHinery asked blankly.

'Nothing.' Ah Wong smiled. 'I thought you might be a linguist.' He picked up a telephone and spoke quickly in Cantonese, referring to the manifest from time to time and ticking off items with a pencil, then replaced the phone. He smiled again. 'Just ordering up some meat and vegetables from my go-down, Mr MacHinery. From your own cargo.'

'And the very cream of the crop, I'll be bound,' MacHinery said bitterly. 'Nae bloody flies on you Chinese.'

Ah Wong smiled yet again. The kind of smile, MacHinery thought grimly, that you might expect to see on the face of a spider when a particularly juicy fly landed on its web. Ah Wong, for his part, thought it unnecessary to inform MacHinery that he was of pure Armenian stock and had changed his name partly for business reasons in a Chinese-dominated field of commerce, but mainly because he regarded the honourable name of his ancestors as sullied beyond redemption by its frequent inclusion in Interpol files throughout the world.

'No need to be bitter, Mr MacHinery,' Ah Wong said pleasantly. 'I thought you might like to stay for dinner with me.'

'Dinner?' After a brief struggle, a conciliatory smile appeared on MacHinery's face. 'Well, noo, Mr Wong, that is kind of you. Very, very kind. I'll be honoured to accept.' MacHinery hadn't sat down again, and now he paced the room restlessly, the sheen of sweat bathing his entire face. He was shivering more violently than ever and one side of his face had begun to twitch.

'You are not well, I'm afraid,' Ah Wong said again.

'I'm fine.' A pause. 'Dammit, no, I'm no'. I'll hae to go oot for a minute to get some medicine. I – I know the cure for this.' He gulped. 'I feel sick, Mr Wong, awful sick. Where's your bathroom? Quick.'

'Through that door there.'

MacHinery left abruptly and closed the door behind him. He turned on both basin taps, pulled the lever that operated the toilet cistern and used the sound of running water to drown the slight clicking noise made as he lifted the Venetian blind that shut out the hot Malayan sun.

Parked on the opposite side of the street below was a dark van with blue-tinted side windows and a ventilator on top. The ventilator was motionless. MacHinery thrust out a hand, waved briefly, withdrew his hand, waited until he saw the ventilator revolve just once, then lowered the blind as cautiously as he had raised it. He turned off the taps and went back into Ah Wong's apartment.

'You feel better, Mr MacHinery?' It was no light task for Ah Wong to get concern into both voice and face but he made it after a struggle.

'I feel bloody awful,' MacHinery said candidly. He was shaking now like a broken bed-spring and his teeth were beginning to chatter. 'I must go oot, Mr Wong. I must. Ma medicine. I'll no be but minutes.'

'Any medicine you care to name, Mr MacHinery, I have it. Among other things, I'm the wholesale supplier to many chemists' shops.'

'You'll no' find the medicine I need in any bloody chemist's shop,' MacHinery said violently. 'A jiffy, Mr Wong. That's all I'll be.' He headed for the doorway, then stopped abruptly. There was a man standing there. By courtesy definition, MacHinery thought, he might be called a man. He looked more like the early prototype of the Neanderthal caveman, only bigger. Much bigger. He had shoulders like a bull, hands like two bunches of bananas and a brutalized moronic face that might have been carved from granite by a power-chisel.

'John,' Ah Wong introduced him. 'My secretary. I don't think he wants you to leave, Mr MacHinery.'

'Aye. Your secretary. No mistaking the intellectual type, is there?' MacHinery shuddered violently again and dropped his voice. 'One side, laddie.'

'Don't be foolish,' Ah Wong said sharply. 'He can break you in half. Come now, Mr MacHinery. Just sit down and take your coat off. Madness to wear it in this heat and sweating as you are.'

'I'm allergic to sunlight,' MacHinery said between clamped teeth. 'Never take it off. One side, you.'

'There's no sunlight in here,' Ah Wong said softly.

'I must get oot,' MacHinery shouted. 'I must. Damn you, Wong, you don't know what you're doing to me.' He made a bull rush for the doorway and tried to dive under John's outstretched arms. His head and shoulders smashed into a five-barred gate. At least, it felt like a five-barred gate. A couple of power shovels closed over MacHinery's upper arms, lifted him effortlessly off his feet and bore him back to the armchair in the centre of the room.

'You are extremely foolish,' Ah Wong said sadly. 'I want to be your friend, Mr MacHinery. And I want you to be mine. I think, Mr MacHinery, that you can offer me what a man in my position so very rarely acquires – an unswerving allegiance that neither money nor oaths could buy.'

MacHinery struggled futilely in the grip of giant hands. He said in a strangled voice: 'I'll kill you for this, Wong.'

'Kill me? Kill your doctor? Kill the one man who can give you the medicine you need?' Ah Wong smiled. 'You are singularly lacking in intelligence. Take his jacket off, John.'

John removed MacHinery's jacket. He did it by the simple process of ripping the white lining down the back middle seam and pulling off the two separate halves.

'Now the shirt sleeves,' Ah Wong murmured.

John twitched his fingers, the buttons burst from their moorings and the sleeves were pulled up beyond MacHinery's elbows. For a long moment all three men stared down at the inside of MacHinery's forearms. Both of them were covered by a mass of pale-purplish spots, none of them more than half an inch distant from its fellows. Ah Wong's face remained as immobile as ever. He bent over MacHinery's Gladstone bag, flung a shirt to one side and picked up a narrow rectangular box. He slid a catch, opened the wooden lid and extracted a hypodermic syringe, holding it by the plunger.

'So very conveniently to hand,' he said gently. 'Your medicine goes in this, doesn't it, MacHinery? And there's hardly a place left in your arms for you to use it, is there? A junky, Mr MacHinery. A dope addict. And now you're climbing the walls, as they say, because you're overdue your next shot. Isn't that it, Mr MacHinery?'

'I'll kill you for this, Ah Wong.' MacHinery's voice was weak, mechanical. He was jerking violently in his seat. 'So help me God, I'll kill you.' He arched himself stiffly in his armchair, his eyes showing white, his mouth strained opened. 'I'll kill you,' he croaked.

'Kill me?' Ah Wong asked quietly. 'Kill the goose that lays the golden eggs? Kill your doctor, as I said before? Kill the doctor who not only recognizes all the symptoms but can prescribe the medicine for it? Prescribe it and supply it. Supply it now. Heroin, is it not, Mr MacHinery?'

John's grip eased. MacHinery struggled to his feet and gripped Ah Wong by the arms. 'You have the stuff?' he whispered. 'God, you have the stuff? You have it here?'

'I have it here.' Ah Wong looked into the stricken eyes. 'My friend Benabi. He is even more brilliant than I had thought. Always the weak link in our organization was the courier from Djakarta to here. But not any more. You will have as much of the white powder, Mr MacHinery, as often as you like, whenever you like, for the remainder of your days.'

'You mean – you mean I'll never have to worry aboot it again? Never have to lie or beg or cheat or steal to get it? It will always be there?'

'While you remain in the employment of Benabi and myself, it will always be there.'

'I'm your man for life,' MacHinery said simply.

'I don't doubt it.' Ah Wong looked at him in distaste, shook off his hands, picked up the phone and spoke rapidly. He replaced the phone and said: 'One minute. No more.'

'My God!' MacHinery said stupidly. 'When I think of the number of times I've chased roond Singapore, near screaming ma head off for the stuff, wondering where I could lay ma hands on it, where the source of supply was, I could – '

'You're at the source now, Mr MacHinery. No need to wonder any more.'

'You – you supply the whole town?'

'Much of it.'

'But – but have you never worried aboot whit you're doing? Have you ever seen a man, a far gone junky, who canna get the stuff? Or a man trying to dry oot? Both going mad. Insane screaming mad. Have you never seen it?'

'Don't be so naive, Mr MacHinery. Of course I've seen it. The sensible ones stick to a pellet of opium. But the sophisticates –' his lips curled – 'must have it straight. If I don't supply it, others will.' He smiled contemptuously. 'Now perhaps you'd like to inform the police?'

'I'll cut ma throat,' MacHinery whispered. 'I'll blow ma brains oot. But I'll never, never tell.'

'I know you won't,' Ah Wong said drily. 'Ah, here it comes.' A servant crossed to the table and dumped a crate of vegetables on top of it.

'Cauliflowers?' MacHinery said stupidly.

'Best Bandung,' Ah Wong agreed. He lifted one, gingerly slit the heart with a knife, extracted a twist of cellophane and poured a little white powder into MacHinery's trembling hand. 'Try it.'

MacHinery placed it on his tongue, tasted it, tasted it again, then whispered: 'Dear God. This is it. This is it. And – and this is the way it comes into Singapore?'

'For years,' Ah Wong said calmly. 'An ordinary cauliflower, the heart carefully parted, the heroin inserted, shellac for preservative and to glue the stems together then carried in the crates. Three times the customs have searched the *Grasshopper* from stem to stern – but who would ever think of cauliflowers?'

'Damn the cauliflowers,' MacHinery said hoarsely. His voice shook, his hands trembled more violently than ever. 'Mix it up for me, for God's sake!'

Ah Wong nodded, went to the bathroom and returned in a minute with a small vial of milky liquid. He nodded to the syringe lying on the table. 'Your medicine, Mr MacHinery.'

'For pity's sake fill the hypo for me,' MacHinery begged. 'My hands – '

'I can see them,' Ah Wong said. 'Unsteady, we might say.' He lifted the hypodermic, depressed the plunger and inserted the needle in the vial. 'Sufficient, I should say, Mr MacHinery?'

'Aye, aye, that'll do.' MacHinery grabbed the hypodermic by the plunger, hesitated, then blurted out: 'God alone knows I'm just a junky, but a man still has his pride. Even a junky. The – the bathroom. And I feel sick again.'

'You make *me* sick,' Ah Wong said dispassionately. 'Go on.'

MacHinery hurried into the bathroom, pulled the cistern lever, opened the Venetian blind and thrust the hypodermic out of the window. Five men came swarming out of the van below. MacHinery withdrew his arm and, still holding the hypodermic gingerly by the plunger, laid it carefully on the windowsill. He waited twenty seconds then walked back into Ah Wong's apartment just as the outer door crashed open and the five men from the van, uniformed policemen with guns, burst into the room. MacHinery nodded towards John.

'Watch the big lad,' he advised. 'If he twitches an eyebrow, shoot five or six bullets into him. Not at his head – they'd bounce off.'

Ah Wong stood stock-still, his face inscrutable. After a moment or two he said softly: 'What is the meaning of this outrage?'

'Inspector Hanbro,' the leading policeman introduced himself. 'Warrant for your arrest, Mr Wong. Receiving, being in illegal possession of and distributing knowingly proscribed narcotics. I have to warn you – '

'What tomfoolery is this?' Ah Wong's face had gone very stiff, very watchful. 'What wild rubbish – narcotics, you said?'

'Narcotics, I said.' Hanbro turned towards MacHinery. 'This man will testify – '

'This man,' Ah Wong said incredulously. 'This derelict Scots engineer – '

'Curiously enough, he was an engineer once,' Hanbro said. 'Also Scots. Hardly derelict. Changed his profession years ago. Mr Wong, may I introduce Inspector Donald MacHinery of the Hong Kong Vice Squad? Seconded to Singapore for – ah – special duties. The faces of my own men are too well known in those parts.'

'You can take him away, Inspector Hanbro,' MacHinery said tiredly. 'I don't know how many wrecked lives and suicides lie at his door and it doesn't matter any more. We have enough on him to put him away for life.'

'I'm innocent of all charges,' Ah Wong said dully. 'As one of the biggest merchants and most influential citizens in – '

'Shut up,' MacHinery said shortly. 'You were right, Mr Wong. Your former courier, the previous chief engineer on the *Grasshopper*, *was* your weak link. He got drunk one night in Djakarta and talked too much in the presence of a plain-clothes man. Just enough for a lead, no more. We knew he wouldn't talk – men who talk in your business invariably die before the night is out – so we let

him be while I established myself on the water-
front as a drunken junky engineer. When the time
was right the Djakarta cops picked him up and
held him incommunicado and there I was waiting,
the ideal substitute. Your pal Benabi wasn't even
smart, far less brilliant.'

'You can't prove a thing. You can't – '

'We can prove everything. Ten years in Hong
Kong and I talk Cantonese as well as you do.
Better – you Armenians have difficulty with some
vowel sounds. Yes, Armenian, Mr Wong – we
know all about you. I heard you give the numbers
to your go-down – they will correspond exactly to
the numbers on the crate.'

'It's only your word – '

'The police had your line tapped, for good
measure.'

'Tapping is inadmissible evidence – '

'And,' MacHinery went on remorselessly,
'every word of our conversation is preserved for
posterity. The bottom half of that Gladstone bag of
mine – a very efficient recorder, I can tell you.
Further, the marks you made on that manifest will
match the crate numbers removed from your go-
down. Graphite tests will show that it was the
pencil on that table that made the marks and fin-
gerprint tests will show that you were the last to
handle that pencil. That signet seal shared by
yourself and Benabi – any court in the East will
recognize the significance of that. That crate there,

lying on your own floor, with dope in every cauli-flower head – how are you going to explain that away? Good lord, man, there's even enough evidence in the bathroom to have you put away for life – a hypo full of heroin with your fingerprints all over the glass cylinder.'

'You're a junky yourself.' Ah Wong's voice was a dazed whisper. 'Narcotics addicts can't testify. I – I know all the symptoms. You – '

'Symptoms?' MacHinery smiled. 'I've already stopped shivering. No bother. And as soon as I remove the three jerseys under my shirt I'll stop sweating, too. Pale face – makeup. Junky's eyes – didn't you know red peppers give exactly the same effect?'

'But your arms,' Ah Wong said desperately. 'Look at them. Riddled with punctures. How –'

'Sharpened knitting needle sterilized and dipped in aniline dye. Don't ever try it, Mr Wong. It's most damnably painful.'

Lancastria

The Tillyer family had come a long, long way. Not so long, perhaps, in terms of actual miles – a moderately fast car could have covered the distance between the Fairey Aviation factory in Belgium, where Clifford Tillyer had worked as a technician, and the port of St Nazaire, in a day. But the Tillyers hadn't travelled across the smiling peacetime plains of Northern France in a fast and comfortable car: they had travelled, instead, across the war-torn chaos of a newly capitulated country, a country where demoralization, for the moment, was as complete as the defeat: and they had travelled either in overcrowded, haphazardly-routed refugee trains that sometimes covered only a few miles a day, or in the backs of trucks that crawled slowly along roads packed with thousands of refugees fleeing to the south.

The journey had taken a long, miserable month, but they had arrived at last: and as Clifford Tillyer, with his wife Vera and two-year-old baby daughter Jacqueline gazed out across the St Nazaire roads, crowded with Allied shipping which ranged from tiny minesweepers to great ocean-going liners all waiting to embark them and take them home to England, he felt that it had all been a hundred times worth while. The suffering, the fear, the privations of hunger and long sleepless nights all lay safely behind: before lay hope and freedom and home.

So, too, felt tens of thousands of others. No civilian refugees these others, but the last regiments of the British Expeditionary Force to France. Most of the BEF had already been evacuated from the continent. The miracle of Dunkirk was a fortnight old, and almost a third of a million men from these beaches were now safely home in England. Cherbourg, St Malo and Brest had been completely evacuated – a fantastic achievement in which 85,000 men had been snatched from the closing pincers of the Panzer divisions without the loss of a single ship or man. And now these men waiting along the banks of the Loire were almost the last to go. Men like Corporal John Broadbent, who had spent almost six weeks driving his OC from Rheims to the evacuation port and whose picture, published in the newspapers of the world, was soon to be known to countless millions: or like Sergeant George Young of the RASC, leaning against the brand new French bicycle which he had trundled half way across France, whose subsequent adventures in the next three days belonged to the realms of the wildest fiction.

But for Sergeant Young and Corporal Broadbent, the past, as it was for the Tillyers, was forgotten. The excitement of the immediate present, the promise that their turn would soon come for one of the dozens of tiny trawlers and minesweepers that were ferrying both soldiers and civilians out to the big ships lying offshore – these were all that mattered. Already they had been told the name of – and could clearly see – the ship that was to take them home: the *Lancastria*. Even at the distance of three or four miles she looked gigantic, massive and solid and secure: once aboard that ship, they told themselves, all their troubles would be over.

The *Lancastria*, a 16,243 ton Cunard White Star liner, swung gently from her two bow anchors in the Quiberon roads as the scores of small craft fussed busily around her during all that long morning and early afternoon of 17 June, 1940. Steadily the complement of soldiers and civilian refugees aboard her mounted – one thousand, two thousand, three thousand, then four. And still the ferryboats came, the numbers mounted, the decks rang constantly to the disciplined tramp of hundreds of marching feet going to their allotted positions in the ship.

Captain R Sharp, watching the scene from the bridge of the *Lancastria*, was desperately anxious for the loading to be finished and the *Lancastria* to be gone. With both anchors down, neither the room nor the ability to manoeuvre the great passenger liner, surrounded by small boats and with the number of refugee troops and civilians aboard steadily mounting with the passing of every minute, he realized all too clearly the hopelessness of offering any organized resistance to aerial or submarine attack.

Submarines, perhaps, were not greatly to be feared – a flotilla of destroyers prowled the estuary unceasingly. But an air attack was another thing: only the previous day the *Franconia* had been attacked and hit, an adumbration, Captain Sharp feared, of worse things still to come. And now again the Luftwaffe's heavy bombers were beginning to launch scattered attacks against the passenger ships in the roads.

But however acute Captain Sharp's apprehensions, however sharp his anxiety for what might befall his ship, he could never have guessed, never have suspected that the name *Lancastria*, then known only to a comparative few, would within a few short days become the worldwide symbol of the greatest maritime disaster in British history, a tragedy worse even than that of the *Titanic*, the *Lusitania* or the *Athenia*.

Half past three in the afternoon. Air-raid sirens were sounding, anti-aircraft guns were beginning to open up against the heavy bombers of the Luftwaffe circling lazily above the Quiberon roads, as the last refugees were just embarking on the *Lancastria* – a total complement, now, of almost 6,000 men, women and children.

Among the six thousand were the Tillyers, Corporal Broadbent and Sergeant Young.

Mrs Tillyer had already bathed, dried and dressed young Jacqueline and now, with her husband and daughter, had gone down to the dining saloon for a meal. What Mrs Tillyer remembers most clearly about that moment was the order and courtesy she found on every hand: the smooth, calm efficiency of the white-jacketed stewards who moved about their duties as if quite oblivious of the gunfire and sirens above: the smiling painstaking care of the sailor who adjusted the tapes of Jacqueline's lifebelt, so that it would no longer slip over the slender shoulders.

Sergeant Young had come aboard almost at the same time as the Tillyers, still lugging his new French bicycle. Ex-Sergeant Young, now living in Wickersley Road, London, admits, in a masterly understatement, that the crew of the over-crowded liner did not take too kindly to the bicycle, but he ignored their curses, hauled it aboard, parked it in what he judged to be a relatively safe position, then went below for a shave, only seconds after he had seen the nearby liner *Oransay* struck on the bridge by a bomb. Bombs were disquieting enough, Mr Young says: but the need for a shave was imperative.

There were no half-measures like shaves, for Corporal John Broadbent. Ex-Coporal Broadbent, now a London taxi-driver living in Newport Street, confesses that he was feeling slightly apprehensive just at that moment, not because of the falling bombs or the fact that he was completely undressed and about to step into a bath, but because the door of the bathroom bore the legend 'Officers Only'.

Just after three-thirty, the *Lancastria* was hit by three aerial torpedoes. One struck for'ard and another aft, but it was the third that caused most of the damage and was responsible for much of the subsequent appalling loss of life.

This aerial torpedo, by one chance in a hundred thousand, plummeted straight down the *Lancastria*'s single funnel and exploded with curiously little sound but devastating power in the confined spaces of the boiler room and adjacent underwater compartments, many of them immovably packed with troops for whom there had been no room on the upper deck.

The boiler room was destroyed. Fuel tanks and lines were ruptured and thousands of gallons of oil immediately filmed out over the adjacent waters until the sea round the *Lancastria* was covered in a thick carpet of oil. But, far more terrible was the fate of the men in the underwater compartments: close on five hundred of them, mostly RAF personnel, were blown out through the great jagged hole blasted through the thin, unarmoured sides of the great liner: many were already dead, killed by the concussive impact of the exploding warhead, by great sheets of steel plate wrenched from the sundered bulkheads, by the flying shrapnel that ricocheted blindly, lethally, around the confined spaces in which these men had been standing: many of those who were flung alive into the water survived only to die in choking, coughing agony in the thick oil pumping out from the ruptured tanks and lines immediately behind them.

Already the *Lancastria* was listing heavily and beginning to settle slowly in the water. Even the most inexperienced aboard – and most of them knew nothing of the sea – knew that the *Lancastria* had not long to live.

Hundreds were trapped below decks. In some cases watertight doors were shut fast or, like many other doors, immovably warped by the buckling effect of the explosion. Others were trapped just as effectively by the solid mass of men filling the gangways and ladders leading to the decks above – there was little hope indeed for the last men in the queues below decks. Some of these escaped through portholes, others through loading ports on the ship's side: Father Charles McMenemy, the former Roman Catholic chaplain in Wormwood Scrubs prison, led a group of such trapped men to a loading port some six feet above the water, gave his own life belt to a sergeant-major who couldn't swim, urged all the men into the sea and went himself last of all. No man ever better deserved to survive than Father McMenemy – and survive he did.

The Tillyers, Corporal Broadbent and Sergeant Young were among the lucky ones – those who reached the upper deck in safety. Broadbent and Young had to take their turn with the others, joining the solid queues of soldiers tramping slowly up the steel-ribbed companionway steps to the freedom of the upper decks and the illusory safety that lay beyond.

Mrs Tillyer had a far easier passage. No sooner had she emerged from the dining room with the lifejacketed baby Jacqueline in her arms than a score of voices took up the cry 'Make way for a baby'. And make way for the baby they did, every man pressing back against the side of the companionway to afford clear gangway, even though they knew the ship was sinking under their feet. This they did for every woman and child on the ship: it can never be computed how many men lost their lives because, in standing back to give way to others, they sacrificed those few seconds that made all the difference between living and dying.

The Tillyers, Broadbent and Young, reviewing these few ghastly hours, retain three outstanding memories in common, and that was the first of them – the utter calmness, the kindness, the selfless gallantry of the soldiers and crew. Confusion there was, and haste – these were inevitable: but of panic there was no trace.

But this impression, permanently engraved in the memory though it was, was a fleeting one only: there was no time for more. The air was filled with the staccato crash of AA weapons from every quarter of the roads, a bedlam of sound and smoke: Luftwaffe bombers still cruised overhead, some of them mercilessly raking the now sharply canting decks of the *Lancastria* with machine-gun fire; the steel-tipped bullets swathing through the close-packed ranks of men queuing up for the lifeboats.

First into the lifeboats were the women and children. Clifford Tillyer saw his wife and Jacqueline aboard one of these boats just as it was about to be lowered. He himself then stepped back into the waiting crowd, only to find himself seized by soldiers from a tank regiment and bundled in beside his wife and child. 'Get in, mister,' they told him. 'You've got to look after your youngster.'

But the lifeboat was a refuge as temporary as it was treacherous. Even as it started lowering towards the oil-slicked sea, it began to capsize. Neither of the Tillyers hesitated. Over the side they went and struck away from the sinking ship, Mr Tillyer holding Jacqueline's head above the oil as best he could.

For Sergeant Young and Corporal Broadbent there were no lifeboats. All those that could be lowered had already gone – arid many of these had capsized.

For the first time in many weeks Sergeant Young forgot all about his bicycle. Lather still on his face from the unfinished shave, he made straight for the side and jumped into the water, into the confusion of wreckage and splintered wood and hundreds of men, many of them nonswimmers with neither life jacket nor anything to cling to, struggling in the water. Young knew what happened to people who stayed too close to sinking ships – and the *Lancastria* was sinking foot by foot before his eyes. He struck out furiously to get well clear of the foundering liner, of the lethal suction that would be the death of anyone in the vicinity when she plummeted to the bottom of the Quiberon roads.

Corporal Broadbent was exactly as he had been when he had been preparing to take his bath – completely naked. (He was to remain thus for three long days.) Nothing, he says, ever worried him less than his unclothed state at that moment. With the deck sliding away beneath his feet he ceremoniously shook hands with his friend Sid Keenan – who had actually been in the bath when the *Lancastria* was hit – and dived into the sea.

Then came the moment when the second main impression of the disaster was registered forever on the minds of the two soldiers and the Tillyers – and, indeed, of every one of the thousands who saw it.

Its great propellors breaking free above the water, the *Lancastria* slowly, inexorably, turned over, just before she sunk. Hundreds of soldiers, most of whom presumably were unable to swim, still clung ant-like to the great hull. There was no shouting, no screaming, no sign of fear at all. Instead, they were singing, and singing in perfect unison, 'Roll out the barrel' and 'There'll always be an England', and they were still singing when the waters closed over them. It is little wonder that many of the soldier survivors could never again bring themselves to sing 'Roll out the barrel', the unofficial anthem of the army in the early years of the war.

Corporal Broadbent was one of the nearest to the ship when it went down. He himself has a personal memory, one which, he says, will always haunt him – the face at the porthole. As the *Lancastria* tipped over, Broadbent could see a man trapped in a cabin desperately trying to smash in the thick toughened glass of the scuttle – trying and completely failing. For one brief moment Broadbent caught sight of the terror-stricken face, then the porthole slid beneath the oil-blackened surface of the sea.

And now came perhaps the worst experience of all – fire. Not fire aboard the *Lancastria* – that would have been easy to escape – but fire on the surface of the sea, and for all too many there could be no escape from that. Nor was the fire any accident, but a piece of calculated and cold-blooded callousness for which there can be no forgiveness. In addition to machine-gunning and killing unknown numbers of people in the water – the twenty occupants of one raft, for instance, were completely wiped out by a sustained burst of machine-gun fire – the Luftwaffe pilots began to drop incendiary bombs on the oil-covered sea, and set it on fire.

Oil on fire is the most horrible, the cruellest death known to men. It is death by slow, agonizing torture, by drowning to escape that torture, by incineration of those parts of the body above water in a lung-gasping asphyxiation – for the flames feed on all the life-giving oxygen on the surface of the sea, and a man suffocates in the superheated and lifeless air. But drowning is quiet and simple and almost without pain, and where no hope of escape is left, only a madman would stretch himself out on the shrieking rack of agony a moment longer than was necessary when the means of kindly deliverance lies so close to hand.

The official history of the war at sea professes itself unable to understand why so many people – 2,823 – lost their lives when the *Lancastria* went down, even though the disaster happened in broad daylight in a road crowded with many ships, especially small, manoeuvrable ships which were quickly on the scene – the anti-submarine trawler *Cambridgeshire* alone rescued almost a thousand survivors.

It is difficult to understand this puzzlement: it is remarkable indeed that so many people, about two and a half thousand, were in fact rescued. Most of the ships in the roads were too busy looking after themselves, fighting off the attacks by the Gelrman bombers, and those which did eventually steam to the oil-covered and wreckage-strewn scene of the sinking liner found comparatively few survivors there after the *Cambridgeshire* had gone. Hundreds had died in the initial explosion, as many again were trapped and taken to the bottom locked inside the shattered hull of the *Lancastria*. Hundreds more, still clinging to the hull, were drowned as the liner plunged to the bottom, and of those then in the water alongside, many were either killed by the flame-covered sea or had swam so far and so frantically in search of safety, that they had put themselves outside the radius of search of the immediate rescue operations.

Such were Corporal Broadbent, Sergeant Young and the Tillyer family.

Broadbent, almost unconscious in the water, was rescued by a small craft and then transferred to the *John Holt*, still completely naked – when a newspaperman's camera clicked. He arrived in Plymouth three days later, still without a stitch of clothes on and bemoaning only the fact that he hadn't a pocket to carry the cigarettes he had been given, to find himself famous, and with his picture, the symbol of the disaster of the *Lancastria*, published in newspapers all over the world.

Sergeant Young had found himself clinging to an orange box, one of ten who depended on the same flimsy support. When he was rescued by a French trawler four hours later, only three were left – the other seven had slipped off one by one as their strength failed. He was landed at a convent hospital, nursed by Mrs Joan Rodes – later famous as 'The Angel of St Nazaire' – given a French sailor's uniform, transferred to a military hospital and there told by a German officer that he was a prisoner of war and would be shot if he tried to run away. Sergeant Young didn't quite run away – along with some others he commandeered a Red Cross van, made his way to the coast and was picked up by the destroyer *Punjabi*.

The Tillyers probably spent even longer than Young in the water – their memories are understandably vague on this point. All that Mrs Tillyer can clearly remember is that a soldier gave up his own piece of wood to which he was clinging to give young Jacqueline every chance possible, and that she kept calling 'Baby here', 'Baby here' so often, and so insistently, that, she says Jacqueline took up the cry as though it were a game. '"Baby here", she kept crying after me, until she grew too weak to say it any more.'

But the cries were heard and rescue came – a lifeboat from the destroyer *Highlander.* Neither Mr Tillyer, now a departmental manager with Fairey Aviation in London, nor his wife were, eventually, any the worse for their shocking appearance.

Neither apparently was baby Jacqueline, for the tiny two-year-old who cried 'Baby here, 'Baby here', in the oil-covered waters of Quiberon Bay eighteen long years ago was married on the 5th of July of this year.

McCrimmon and the Blue Moonstones

The wind was blowing offshore from the native quarter, so that breathing, up-town, was only a matter of tolerable difficulty. Night, if not peace, had fallen over the city. The hour was late and all honest citizens were at home, asleep. The streets of Alexandria were thronged.

The scene was typically Eastern. Uncounted thousands were strenuously engaged in their legitimate pursuits of boot-blacking, pocket-picking and the retailing of every conceivable article rigorously proscribed by Egyptian law. But, for the most part, the bulk of the crowds wandered aimlessly, purposelessly around. Some went one way, some another; but whichever way they went, they went only because they happened to be going that way.

But one there was who, although among them, was clearly not of them – one who hastened briskly along, whose every step betrayed the man of action, whose face held that calm set born of fixed determination, whose eye held the bright gleam born of high resolve and, possibly, too much gin. McCrimmon, Able Seaman, torpedo-man aboard His Majesty's Ship *Ilara*, proud possessor of two badges, a distinguished name and a remarkable set of moral principles, had an urgent appointment which would brook no delay.

HMS *Ilara* had arrived back in Alexandria, from the Aegean, only that morning, with a large section of her after-funnel missing – the souvenir of a slight estrangement which had arisen between her and the 9.5 German batteries on Milos. McCrimmon, ruthlessly sacrificing his normal afternoon sleep, had hied him ashore immediately after dinner and sought out a certain Mr McCrimmon, a third, or it may have been fourth cousin of his. Mr McCrimmon was a dockyard worker, or, more precisely, one who was paid for being present in the dockyard at certain stated times. He was not due to go home for almost two years yet. He had newly come, it appeared, into the possession of certain valuable information, and, blood – however diluted – being thicker than water, he had, after due deliberation and several brandies, parted with this to his cousin. The latter had maintained throughout an attitude of detached boredom which had deceived no one.

The information, in brief, was this. He, Mr McCrimmon, had learned, through a devious

but reliable channel, of a certain native ashore who
had rather a fine set of semi-precious stones. That
they were not family heirlooms or otherwise
legally come by, Mr McCrimmon was quite sure;
but that was irrelevant. What was relevant was the
fact that their current owner was prepared to sell
them at a fantastically low price. They would fetch
several times that amount in the inflated home
market. Would his cousin, whom he trusted above
all men and who was due to go home shortly, carry
out this transaction for him and forward fifty per
cent of the proceeds?

His cousin would, and 'tis thus we find him striding through the crowded streets, looking neither
to the left nor to the right, automatically cuffing
all such boot-blacks as came within range and
pausing only occasionally, with a muttered curse,
to study proffered works of art, by old masters and
others, then hastening along again.

His appointment, as mentioned, would brook
no delay. He had already delayed long enough in
a saloon down by the Bourse, slaking his thirst
and playing poker with three Armenians and a
Cypriot. McCrimmon had done very well out of
the game, and might have been there yet, had not
some inquisitive bystander seen fit to comment, in
terms of loud admiration, upon the exquisite del-
icacy of the workmanship whereby the backs of
the cards were painted in fifty-two different

patterns. When an impromptu court of enquiry was set up to investigate the ownership of the cards, McCrimmon had left. He had not even stayed to collect his winnings, a recollection which caused him to grind his teeth from time to time as his feet spurned the dust of the Saad Zaghoul.

Arriving at the further end of this, the main street of the city, he turned left and disappeared into one of the several ornate restaurant cum dance-hall establishments clustered around Ramleh Station. Briskly saluting the commissionaire, whom he took for a rear-admiral, McCrimmon passed within the portals, tightened his grip on hat and coat as he went by the hat-check counter and looked around the vestibule. It was empty. The jewel merchant had not yet arrived.

Leaving a few words of instruction and a still fewer number of piastres with the receptionist, McCrimmon vanished within the restaurant. He chose a table where he could observe the cabaret without undue strain to the eyes and seated himself. Removing the 'Reserved' card on the table, he handed it, with a grandiloquent gesture, to a passing waiter, along with his order for refreshments. The waiter, convinced that he was dealing with yet another exiled king in disguise, bowed low and moved off.

McCrimmon bent a supercilious eye around the restaurant. It was in no way different from a score

of others he knew – the same plush settees, curtained alcoves, brass rails, minute dancing-floor,
tired palms and even more tired string orchestra.

He lackadaisically watched the efforts of a couple
of professional dancers, demonstrating an old-time
waltz. The lurid handbill on his table referred to
them as 'a pair of talented and finished artists'.
McCrimmon questioned the 'talented' but agreed
with the 'finished', privately estimating the date at
twenty years previously. His boredom mounted
apace.

An hour passed. McCrimmon had just lowered
his fifth John Collins, and was waxing impatient,
when a waiter signalled him. The orchestra was
playing 'Carmelita' and, as McCrimmon walked
out, the music harmonized very well with the not
unmelodious tinkling given off by the chromium
ashtray and monogrammed forks and spoons in
his coat pocket.

Pressing a cylindrical disc of some base metal
into the gratified waiter's hand, McCrimmon
emerged into the vestibule. Again there was no one
there, but as the waiter had informed him that
someone awaited him, he pressed through the only
other door, other than the exit, leading off the
vestibule.

Again he drew a blank – in one sense. For,
though the washplace, for such it was, was empty,
McCrimmon's professional attention was drawn to
the row of gleaming chromium taps. He bethought

himself of his uncle, proprietor of a flourishing plumber and gasfitter's firm in the Broomielaw, Glasgow. Muttering some proverb about time lost never being regained, McCrimmon drew forth a ten-inch Stilson wrench, expertly calculated with his eye the gauge of the gland nut on the taps and was adjusting the spanner when a low, sibilant voice behind him said 'Meester!'

McCrimmon started, performed some masterly sleight of hand with the Stilson, then turned unconcernedly round. If innocence of expression were any criterion, any unbiased judge, could he have seen him in company with an average archangel, would have branded the latter as a habitual criminal.

Before him stood, or crouched, a diminutive, dark-skinned individual, clad in a scarlet fez and an off-white nightgown. His feet were bare. To the casual eye, he seemed to be shaking hands industriously with himself; McCrimmon correctly interpreted this as a gesture of propitiation. Again the apparition spoke.

'Meester Creemon?' he enquired.

McCrimmon, deeming it useless to point out the correct pronunciation of a legendary Highland name to the unlettered heathen, merely nodded assent. The native, equally a man of few words, said no more. Beckoning, he turned, slipped out of the doorway, through the vestibule and into the street. McCrimmon, suitably impressed by his conspiratorial air, cast a last regretful glance at the chromium taps, made a mental note to bring a haversack next time and lurked after him.

Satisfied that he was not alone, the native shuffled noiselessly across the square. McCrimmon followed, keeping, as became an upholder of the dignity of Western civilization, several ostentatious paces to the rear. The guide led the way up the rue Safia Zaghoul, over the hill, down the other side and into the native quarter immediately east of the docks.

As the streets grew meaner and darker and the smell more villainous, so did McCrimmon's grip on his wrench tighten. But he did not hesitate. Was he not a McCrimmon? Had not his ancestors done their part nobly and well at Bannockburn and Flodden? Had not, in more recent times, his grandfather run more bootleg hooch throughout the Western Isles than any other man in contemporary history? Had he not seen, with his own eyes, his father, with that cheerful contempt of death so characteristic of the McCrimmons, cheer the Glasgow Rangers to victory whilst imbedded in a solid phalanx of Celtic supporters? There was no lack of glorious precepts. Besides, he had lifted his elbow many times that evening. His courage was as the courage of ten. McCrimmon pressed on.

His guide suddenly stopped before a dilapidated café; outwardly, at least, it was unprepossessing in the extreme. McCrimmon, following the guide through the hanging reeds screening the doorway, found that the outward façade belied the interior, which was considerably worse. It consisted of a bar running the length of the room, half a dozen tables with wicker chairs and a few stools. In one corner, a scruffy individual was toasting a flat loaf over an open brazier. Hard by him two aged gentlemen were squatting on the floor, manfully sucking at a bubbling hookah. McCrimmon could not discern what, if anything, was happening at the other end of the room. Visibility did not exceed four feet.

The guide evidently felt completely at home here. Leading McCrimmon over to a rickety table by the brazier, he sat down and, in a burst of confidence, disclosed himself as one Mohammed Ali. Parenthetically, it may here be remarked that fifty per cent of the male population of Egypt are called Mohammed Ali; the remaining fifty per cent, unambitious souls, are content with calling themselves Mohammed or Ali.

Introductions thus tardily effected, McCrimmon, whom the refinements and social trappings of big business left completely cold, called for drinks and brusquely demanded that they come to business. Mohammed Ali slid a hand into a fold of his robe and drew out a small, wash-leather bag. Weighing this speculatively in his hand, he said nothing, but his enquiring, meaningful glance more than compensated for any lack of words.

McCrimmon demanded to see the stones:
Mohammed Ali declined. Surely the English
Meester would at least demonstrate his good faith
by showing his money. McCrimmon, writhing
under the double insult of the opprobious epithet
'English' and the disrepute into which the word
of a McCrimmon had clearly fallen among the
savage tribes of the East, groped for the handle of
his Stilson.

Mohammed Ali, to whom the higher forms of
etiquette were obviously a closed book, chose this
moment to begin manicuring his hands after his
own unostentatious fashion. His nail-file took the
form of a 9-inch, double-edged throwing knife;
McCrimmon, reflecting that, after all, the rude
and untutored upbringing of these unfortunates
entitled them to pity rather than censure, mag-
nanimously changed his mind about the Stilson
and thrust his hand into his left coat-pocket,
where he kept his wallet. It remained there for a
few seconds, then emerged slowly. His hand was
empty. His face wore a most peculiar expression.
Not to put too fine a point on it, his wallet was
gone.

What ensued would have thrown any aspiring
etymologist into transports of rapture. With every
second word unprintable, McCrimmon anathe-
matized the world in general and Alexandria in
particular for five full minutes without repeating
himself once. He held his audience spellbound.

Finally, he calmed down, soothed by Mohammed Ali's consoling words and several glasses of native-brewed arrack.

After much further argument and bandying of words, it was agreed that they should meet again on the following night, at a café at the hither end of the Sherif Pasha – a rendezvous insisted on by McCrimmon. The advantages were two-fold – it was in the white quarter, and McCrimmon was not unknown there; had they been there that evening, wallet or no wallet, the necessity for a further assignation would not have arisen . . .

McCrimmon sat on for some time, drinking moodily and deciding to leave only when Mohammed Ali showed no signs of supplying any further arrack. Clutching at the wavering bar in an effort to steady it, he rose to go; he wore the weary air of a man whom fate could harm no more. It was, after all, a pardonable assumption.

Launching forth in the general direction of the door, he found it blocked by a quartette who showed no signs of complying with his imperative calls for gangway. Focusing his eyes with considerable difficulty, McCrimmon peered at the nearest of the four; his mind, harking back several leagues, ultimately identified him as the Cypriot to whom he had been demonstrating the finer points of poker earlier on in the evening. Intuition told him who the remaining three gentlemen were.

Shocked into comparative sobriety and hoarsely uttering the war cry of his clan, McCrimmon leapt back. A high-speed camera would have recorded but a blur as his hand streaked for his Stilson wrench. Wild Bill Hickok, at his best, would have stood in silent wonder. Alas for McCrimmon, the miraculous speed of his draw was grievously hampered by the plethora of assorted cutlery in his pocket. True, it caused but a second's delay: but it is a scientifically established fact that a heavy stool, impelled by the arms of an enraged Armenian, can cover a distance of four feet in less than half that time.

A naval patrol happened to be passing by as McCrimmon emerged, in slightly unorthodox fashion, through the closed lattice window of the café. It was an unusual method of exit, but not sufficiently so to warrant investigation by any average hardened naval patrol. Pausing only to separate him from the splintered woodwork festooned around his neck, the patrol picked him up and escorted his tottering form to the sanctuary of the docks.

Dragging himself away from the mirror wherein he had been gazing with rapturous admiration for the past ten minutes, McCrimmon adjusted his hat to the correct angle befitting an Active Service A/B, donned his raincoat, checked up on his armoury and prepared to leave the mess-deck.

It was nightfall on the following day, Sunday. During the morning McCrimmon had held a council of war with his cousin, who was that day accumulating an impressive amount of overtime in 'A' Turret. Annoyed as he initially was by McCrimmon's intrusion – for even the most phlegmatic amongst us resents any interruption of a deep and healthful slumber – his cousin was soon cursing luridly and gnashing his teeth in perfect sympathetic unison with McCrimmon as the latter unfolded his sorry tale. But there were no hard feelings – amongst the McCrimmons, recriminations are quite unknown. Another wallet of notes would be forthcoming by evening. The loss, McCrimmon assured his grateful cousin, could be made good by another two or three overtime weekends, even though he was not the man he was, as he had latterly begun to be troubled by insomnia.

Many a lesser man, in his circumstances and in the light of recent events, would have categorically refused to venture ashore; but there are no lesser men among the McCrimmons. He was watch aboard that night, but had easily circumvented that slight technicality by mortgaging his rum for the next three days to a messmate – a practice strictly at variance with Service regulations, and, therefore, all the more dear to the heart of McCrimmon.

Satisfied that all was well, and that his wallet, only to be used as a last resort, was securely stowed in an inner pocket, he climbed briskly up the rope ladder to the upper deck passage-way. It is here worth recording that the steel ladder, normally in position, had been removed that morning for the purpose of welding new foot-grips on the worn, shiny steps.

He arrived ashore in the liberty-boat some thirty minutes later, passed out of the dock, strode up through the native quarter, rolled his way along the vast cobbles of the rue Soeurs, turned into Mohammed Ali square, crossed it diagonally and disappeared down the Sherif Pasha.

On arrival at the rendezvous, he exchanged a few genial words with the proprietor – an old acquaintance of his – pressed some genuine Egyptian currency into the hands of the two large Yugoslav waiters and seated himself in the private recess curtained off from the restaurant. Here he patiently awaited the arrival of Mohammed Ali, from time to time smiling with smug self-satisfaction and automatically easing the heavy wrench in his pocket.

Ten minutes passed, and Mohammed Ali arrived. He was not alone. The man who followed him in stood about six foot one in his bare feet and was so broad that he found it necessary to turn sideways in order to pass through the door-way. A large man by any standards, he was puny and stunted when compared to the other two dark-skinned individuals who pressed in behind him. Mohammed Ali's companions appeared to have been chosen with a complete lack of the aesthetic viewpoint.

McCrimmon ground his teeth in black fury and bitterly marvelling at the depravity and depths of distrust of human nature, he smiled broadly and greeted Mohammed Ali with a cordiality that would have embarrassed any but the blackest-hearted. Mohammed Ali remained unmoved.

The wrench was hastily pushed well out of sight and the wallet dragged forth from the more remote fastnesses of McCrimmon's clothing. Mohammed Ali, permitting himself the merest smirk, took out the wash-leather bag, unloosened the neck and spilled the contents on the table. There were eighteen stones in all, blue moonstones, small but perfectly matched.

McCrimmon, who probably knew less about precious stones than any other man living, produced a magnifying glass which the Navigator had carelessly left lying around his chart table and proceeded to examine the stones with the hawk-like eye of the Hatton Garden expert.

For a long time he examined them, one by one. He picked each new one up hopefully, scrutinized it and cast it away in a disparaging fashion, carefully allowing his expression of disappointment to deepen after each unspoken condemnation.

Mohammed Ali fidgeted and fumed. McCrimmon ignored him completely.

Mohammed Ali's patience wore very thin. Clearing his throat after his unpleasant fashion, he stated his price as 800 piastres. McCrimmon, rapidly calculating that, on figures supplied by his cousin, this would give him only 500 per cent profit, cast away another moonstone with an even more marked degree of disgust, and laughed hollowly. He had spent much time in practising and bringing to its present state of perfection that hollow laugh of his and it had served him well more than once in the past.

It affected Mohammed Ali not at all. McCrimmon once more gnashed his teeth and offered 500 – a ridiculously high price, but he, McCrimmon, was not the man to haggle over an odd piastre. Neither, apparently, was Mohammed; he restated his original figure and then the haggling began in earnest. Both called for alcoholic sustenance; not, as the innocent might expect, from a spirit of amity but in the fervid, if unChristian, hope that it might cloud the other's intellect.

When McCrimmon left the café a brief two hours later, the blue moonstones were his; his wallet, true, had been lightened to the extent of 500 piastres, but he was more than satisfied with the night's work. Granted, there had been a slightly unpleasant scene when McCrimmon, producing a 1938 Currency Quotation book, had endeavoured to pay in Greek money (rate of exchange, in the year '44, due to inflation, being approximately five million drachmas to the penny); but further reflection, coupled with the sight of one of Mohammed Ali's bodyguards absentmindedly tying knots in a small crowbar, had convinced him of the unwisdom of this. Still, as aforesaid, he was satisfied. McCrimmon decided to celebrate.

Some time after midnight, it was borne in upon McCrimmon that, for every twenty paces he took, he was making no more than one yard's direct progress. Rightly calculating that it would thus take him several hours to cover the mile that separated him from the docks, he hailed a gharry. Mounting, he enthroned himself on the collapsible hood and shouted ironic encouragement to the decrepit Jehu, who uselessly belaboured the ancient collection of skin and bones barely supported by the gharry's shafts.

They arrived at No 14 gate in ten minutes. McCrimmon vaulted gracefully over the side of the gharry and collapsed in an inert heap in the gutter. Picked up and revivified by the army guard, he staggered down to the quay and found that the last liberty-boat had departed three hours previously. He hired a felucca, and his powerful, off-key baritone, rendering the 'Skye Boat Song', reverberated among the silent ships as the two natives laboriously rowed out of the windless inner harbour. In the outer harbour, with sail raised, he switched to 'Shenandoah', and so went through his painfully extensive repertoire, craftily changing to 'Rule Britannia' as the felucca came within earshot of the Officer of the Watch of the *Ilara*.

Making good his escape up the chain ladder while the natives searched the bottom of the boat for the handful of carelessly thrown Glasgow Corporation tramway tokens, McCrimmon made his way for'ard. He disappeared into a convenient patch of blackness which enveloped the port side amidships of the *Ilara*, and tarried there a space while he opened the heavy steel doors of a small compartment and tucked the bag of blue moonstones safely inside. They were completely hidden. He closed the door, tightened the clamps with a tommy bar and departed on his way, smirking widely and fulsomely congratulating himself on his own genius. At no time was McCrimmon's faith in his fellow-man very marked.

He passed within the for'ard screen door and navigated his unsteady way to the hatchway leading down to his mess-deck. Above this hatchway brightly burned a warning red lamp; this he incorrectly judged to be merely yet another of the brightly coloured spots which had been interfering with his vision for some little time. Swinging his leg over the coaming, McCrimmon started to descend the ladder with the careless aplomb of the born sailor; it was not until he recovered consciousness several hours later in the Sick Bay that he recollected that the ladder had been removed the previous day.

On the following day the *Ilara* left for operational duties. Three days later McCrimmon was well on the highroad to recovery and on the fourth he suffered a serious relapse.

About 7.00 am on the fourth morning, the *Ilara* intercepted and sunk a small German transport evacuating troops from Crete. McCrimmon had heard the news and had been not unaware of desultory gunfire. About 10.00 am he summoned the Sick Berth Attendant and lackadaisically asked for details. He was told that the trooper had been disabled by gunfire and, when emptied of troops, sunk by torpedo.

Insofar as it was possible for a complexion the colour of saddle-leather to match a snow-white pillow, McCrimmon's now did just this. Finding some difficulty with his breathing, he asked the SBA whether he knew which tubes had been used. The SBA did and informed him that the port ones were the ones in question. The SBA was now thoroughly alarmed, as he had it on the best authority that only dying men plucked the coverlet after the fashion his patient was now using.

Moaning slightly, McCrimmon mustered the last tattered shreds of the legendary McCrimmon courage and feebly enquired whether the torpedo which had done the deadly deed had issued from X, Y or Z. 'Ah! no, no, not X.' 'Yes – X.'

As the first wave of kindly oblivion swept over his shattered frame, McCrimmon momentarily and agonizingly relived those few moments of inspired cunning – now clearly seen for the maniacal folly that it was – when he had stowed the moonstones inside X torpedo tube. With the fleeting realization that 'jewel-studded Aegean' was no longer the empty phrase that it had been in Byron's time, McCrimmon lapsed into a stunned unconsciousness which caused the SBA to have no hesitation whatsoever in calling both medical officers at once.

Physically speaking, McCrimmon eventually made a complete recovery: mentally, he is scarred for life. More terrible still, internecine warfare has at last destroyed the historic solidarity of the Clan McCrimmon. I met McCrimmon the other day, striding briskly along Glasgow's Argyll Street, with an empty haversack over his shoulder – he had just been on a visit to his plumber uncle in the Broomielaw – and he told me sadly that, even after the lapse of years, his cousin was still looking for him.

They Sweep the Seas

It was still night when we cast off and nosed our way through the outer harbour, crammed with vessels of all sizes and nationalities, riding peacefully at anchor. Cold, grey rain was sluicing down mercilessly, spattering off our deck and churning the murky water to a light foam, and from the bridge, visibility scarcely extended beyond the trawler's bows. We felt, rather than saw, our way out to the open sea, barely making headway. We brushed along the side of a sister trawler, and farther on felt our hull scraping over an anchor cable, the black hulk of the ship's bows looming perilously near. Approaching the entrance, and feeling reasonably safe, we increased speed, and all but collided with a big Finnish freighter, which had worked with the tide across the harbour mouth; it was the word 'SUOMI', painted in six-foot high letters, gleaming whitely through the darkness, that gave us warning. Our skipper cursed fluently, spun the wheel to starboard, and we passed on. But we reached the sea without mishap.

In the harbour, it had been comparatively warm and sheltered, but a very different state of affairs existed beyond the headland. The trawler pitched wickedly in the long, heavy rollers coming in from the Atlantic, drenching itself in spray. Sometimes an exceptionally heavy sea foamed along fo'c'sle high, poured into the well, slid over the deck, and went gurgling through the scuppers; but this did not happen often. The wind was not strong, but possessed that biting quality which makes one raise one's coat collar and withdraw, hurriedly, to the lee-side of the upper deck. There are few bleaker and more cheerless places than the west coast of Scotland in the early morning of a January day.

As the trawler went butting through the seas, in the chill grey of the breaking dawn, to its appointed station, the two officers on the bridge discussed the prospects of the coming sweep. Both agreed that it would be a trying day, that it would be as boring as ever, and that they would, as usual, encounter no mines. They disagreed, however, concerning the weather: the Lieutenant thought there was little chance of the wind dying down or the weather moderating; but the skipper was of the opinion that both would come to pass, although, probably, later in the day.

Neither the Lieutenant nor the skipper was a young man. The Lieutenant (RNR) wore three rows of ribbon, had been in the Dardanelles in the last war, and walked with a pronounced limp – a memento of Zeebrugge. He had retired ten years ago, but at the outbreak of war had left his comfortable, even luxurious, existence for the unknown perils and hardships of a minesweeper's existence. He did not do this as a favour to his country: he did it as his duty.

The Lieutenant, as has been said, was not a young man, but the skipper was at least ten years older. Half a century had passed since he first went down to the sea. He had swept mines in the war of 1914–18, but had considered himself, not unnaturally, too old for such an arduous task in this. Then one day, while trawling in the North Sea, he had been bombed and machine-gunned by a Heinkel. The bombs had missed, but the bullets had literally riddled one of his crew. That man was his son. And so he had changed his mind about being too old.

An hour after clearing the harbour mouth, we reached the beginning of our beat and cut the engines until the trawler had barely enough way to keep head on to the seas. We were awaiting the arrival of our companion sweeper, who made her appearance some ten minutes later, pitching heavily up on our starboard quarter, a vague shape in the dim half-light.

We drifted a light line astern and she altered her course to port, to pick it up. A wire was attached to this; we hauled it aboard our own trawler, attached the sweep wire to it, and paid it out astern again. At regular intervals, peculiarly shaped objects, professionally known as 'kites', were shackled to the hawser by two seamen, whose stoic features betrayed no signs of the extreme discomfort they must have been experiencing from their raw hands and stiff, cold-benumbed fingers. These 'kites' acted as weights upon the sweep wire, keeping it at the requisite distance beneath the surface of the water.

No landlubber or 'freshwater' man could have performed this task of paying out the sweep wire; it was an operation that demanded the very highest standards of seamanship. The co-ordination and sense of timing of the man at the wheel, the two 'shacklers', and, above all, the winch-driver, were marvellous to a degree. They worked as smoothly and as swiftly as the well-oiled, correlated cogs of an intricate machine.

Everything adjusted to his satisfaction, our Lieutenant signalled, by siren, to the other trawler that he was ready to commence his sweep. She acknowledged his signal, swept round to our starboard beam, and off we went, beating southwards. It was becoming rougher, and the Lieutenant, studiously avoiding the skipper's eye, was smiling with ill-concealed satisfaction. It was not often that the skipper's weather forecasts proved false, but this time, for once, he seemed to have slipped up.

We were broadside on to the seas now, one moment lifting over a sullen, spume-capped crest, the next sliding along a shallow trough, clouds of icy spray cascading inboard. The pitching had given place to a rather unpleasant rolling motion, the latter being a decided change for the worse. It was now that the genius – and genius it was – of the winch-driver asserted itself. His job it was to see that the sweep wire did not become too slack, which would have been bad enough, or become too taut, which might have resulted in tragedy. Sailors have, with good reason, a holy dread of overstrained hawsers. A snapped wire is a lethal weapon, and its power of destruction is rather terrifying; such a wire can slice off a man's head far more efficiently than the sharpest axe. But, judging from our winch-driver's nonchalance and the deceptively careless ease with which he manipulated the levers, one would have thought that no such unpleasant possibility had ever occurred to him.

On the bridge, the Lieutenant was poring over a minutely detailed Admiralty chart spread open before him. Also consulting it, but with a much lesser degree of concentration, was the skipper, who only did it that he might not hurt the feelings of the Lieutenant, for whom he entertained a very high regard. Privately, however, he held Admiralty charts and all such inessentials in a mighty contempt, and considered them unworthy of a real sailor. He had never needed a chart; a torn, finger-stained school atlas had served his purpose equally well.

When the Lieutenant judged we had reached the end of our beat, he pulled on the siren lanyard, and the other trawler cut her speed down to a mere crawl; whereas we continued at full speed and came sweeping round in a full half-circle, a manoeuvre which, though apparently simple, like all else in minesweeping, was, in actuality, a brilliantly executed bit of seamanship. One might have been excused for thinking that we had been hauled round by centripetal force, our companion trawler acting as the pivot and the sweep wire as the connecting link, so high a state of perfection had the co-ordination existing between the two trawlers reached.

All morning we continued in this fashion, beating up and down and gradually working our way westward. The wind, in the meantime, had veered from the west to north-by-west, and, though not becoming any stronger, had become exceedingly cold. At this juncture, we began to feel truly sorry for the winchman, exposed, as he was, to the full force of the elements, but consoled ourselves with the thought that he was specially adapted for resisting the cold, owing to his enormous girth. We were surprised to learn, however, that he was of normal proportions but wore no fewer than five overcoats under his oilskins and life jacket. But this may merely have been malicious rumour and we never received any confirmation as to its truth. Suffice is it to say that his attitude, regarding the weather, of the completest unconcern was Spartan to a degree.

If he was, undeniably, the most important member of the crew, the second most, equally without doubt, was the cook. Balancing himself with a marvellous agility, born of long and arduous practice, he made his appearance at regular intervals – never exceeding three-quarters of an hour – bearing, in the one hand, a large and much-battered iron kettle, and in the other, a motley assortment of tin mugs, joined together by a strand of wire passed through their handles. The kettle was filled, alternately, with strong, sweet tea and cocoa, and the contents surpassed, we were of the opinion, anything we had ever experienced in the finest of city restaurants. Apparently coffee does not find favour in the eyes of the crews of minesweepers.

Minesweeping is a dreadfully monotonous business, but we managed to pass the time tolerably well by smoking, spinning yarns, and drinking the cook's concoctions. In the early morning, a huge, four-engined flying boat of the Coastal Command passed directly overhead, acknowledging our humble presence by dipping graciously in salute, at which we felt highly flattered. About noon, a small convoy appeared on the southern horizon, but was gone within half an hour. Occasionally, gulls or wild duck flew overhead, and twice we saw the round, black, glistening head of a particularly venturesome seal emerge from a nearby wave, stare at us coldly and dispassionately, after the manner of its kind, then sink beneath the waves with an expression of disgust on its face. But noteworthy incidents were non-existent, and we gradually settled down into a state of wakeful boredom.

About two o'clock in the afternoon, when conversation had languished and died, and we were conjuring up fanciful visions of what we should have for our evening meal, our dreams were abruptly shattered by a loud, incoherent, but unmistakably triumphant cry from our indefatigable winch-driver. We dashed to the starboard side of our vessel and scanned the stretch of water under which the sweep wire was passing, eagerly awaiting the first appearance of the mine – as mine it must be. We could see nothing: neither had our winch-driver seen anything, but he had *felt* some foreign body making contact with the sweep wire – and he was far too experienced a man to make a mistake.

It was a tense moment, holding, as it did, two distinct possibilities regarding the immediate future of the mine – one unpleasant, the other not so. (Parenthetically, it speaks well for our faith in our winch-driver that we never doubted the existence of the mine.) In the first case, our sweep wire might foul the detonating mechanism of the mine, which would forthwith blow up, in which event our sweep wire would be almost inevitably destroyed. Moreover, we had no means of knowing how close the mine was to one or other of our trawlers, and it was far from improbable that the explosion of the mine would entail our own or our companion sweeper's destruction. Such things had happened before. The other, and infinitely more pleasing possibility was that the mine would be drawn on to one of the cutters, be severed from its anchorage, and float harmlessly to the surface. To our immense relief, it was the latter that came to pass.

At a spot that was almost mathematically equidistant between the two trawlers, the mine rose slowly to the surface and remained there, rising and falling sluggishly with the seas, an evil-looking, murderous spheroid of black steel, about three feet in diameter, liberally covered with knobs. These knobs, when broken, set the detonating mechanism in action and explode the mine. We steamed on for some distance farther, in order to carry the sweep well out of the mine's reach, and, almost before we had stopped, two of the crew had their rifles out and were firing at the mine, patently bent on its early despatch and eager to witness the explosion and its spectacular after-effects. In their laudable efforts they were nobly supported by the crew of the other trawler.

After about a score of ineffectual shots had been fired by each trawler, it became evident that the disposal of the mine was going to be a by no means simple matter. The heaving decks of the trawlers, combined with the fact that the target was not static, made for very inaccurate shooting. Still, persistency had its own due, if not very satisfying, reward, for, after another ten minutes, the mine sank to the floor of the sea, riddled with bullets, none of which had the luck to impinge on any of the detonators. Although our object had been accomplished and the mine rendered harmless to shipping, one and all were grievously disappointed at the mine's inglorious end, having been pardonably desirous of witnessing a more dramatic finale. With a glow of inward satisfaction, not unmixed with a slight feeling of frustration, we returned to our posts and resumed operations.

Contrary to popular conception, minesweepers do not sweep up and explode dozens of mines every day. Long weeks may pass without so much as the sight of a mine; this was, accordingly, a red-letter day for the crew of our trawler. We had already nine white-painted chevrons adorning our long black funnel, signifying that we had destroyed that number of mines; already the ship's artist was ferreting out his paint and brush, preparatory to painting our tenth chevron when we should reach port or the weather moderate sufficiently to permit of it.

Towards evening the skies began to clear, the wind backed round to the westward again, and the rough, wind-swept seas gradually calmed down to a gentle swell. If the Lieutenant felt chagrined at his interrupted success as a weather prophet, he concealed his feelings remarkably well; probably, however, the excitement and success of the early afternoon had driven all thought of it from his mind. Some time later the cloud-banks to the west lifted, and, for the first time that day, we saw the sun, an enormous ball of dull red, its circumference very clearly etched through the low-lying winter haze.

Half an hour later, the sun dipped slowly below the southwestern horizon, laying a broken path of crimson over the sea of our ship. Soon after, as the light was failing and we had the better part of twenty miles to go before we reached our home port, the Lieutenant signalled to our companion trawler to cease operations and disconnect the sweep wire. We hauled it aboard, unshackled the 'kites' and stowed them carefully away; we then turned the trawler's bows towards the east, for the first time that day, and set a course for home through the swiftly gathering darkness.

The day's work was done. The skipper, his hands gently caressing the wheel, was talking quietly to the Lieutenant, relaxed on a disreputable camp stool, his back against the bulkhead, his hands behind his head. Down below, the cook, his labours over, was lying on his bunk, reading a detective novelette. The winch-driver, impervious, as ever, to the icy wind which still blew, had not stirred from his post, but was dreamily regarding our slightly phosphorescent wake, watching it recede gradually into the darkness. A couple of men were sheltering from the following wind in the well-deck before the bridge, quietly smoking. Yet another two men were on the bridge-deck, steadying a ladder, on the top of which was perched a man for whom the slight pitching of the ship, the insufficient light, and the chilly night wind were proving no deterrent in the execution of his task. To him, art was all. He was painting our tenth chevron on the funnel . . .

Words cannot adequately express what we owe to these men – fishermen all, from the Hebrides and Mallaig, Wick and Peterhead, Aberdeen and Grimsby, Lowestoft and Yarmouth. Call them heroes, and they would jeer at you: yet they are nothing else. Theirs is, at once, the most lonely, monotonous, and dangerous of all our Empire Forces' tasks, and one indispensable for the maintenance of danger-free sea-lanes for the Merchant Service, our lifeline with the world beyond. They put to sea in the morning, gay or grave according to their wont . . . and some do not return. But they close their ranks, and carry on.

City of Benares

Colin Ryder Richardson, a city broker, and
Kenneth Sparks, a Post Office employee, both live
in the western outskirts of London, the former in
Worcester Park, Surrey, the latter in Alperton,
Middlesex. Both are approximately the same age,
both are married, both have a baby son.
Superficial similarities, these, similarities that
could be duplicated ten thousand times: but
through the warp and woof of the lives of these
two young men runs a coloured thread of memory that sets them apart from all the others: the
memory of that dark and bitter and hopeless night
eighteen long years ago, when the torpedoed liner
City of Benares slid beneath the gale and sleet-torn
surface of the North Atlantic and left them to die
in the cold and hostile waters.

They should have died that night. Their
chances of survival, the chances of survival of any
child, in waters such as these, were remote. But

incredibly survive they did – they and a handful of other children. A handful, no more. The chances were remote, and with the sinking of the *City of Benares*, a tragedy which aroused more pity and indignation than any other naval loss of the war, the law of averages had its inexorable way. Of the hundred young children aboard the liner, no less than eighty-three, far from the parents, the homes, and the friends that had until then made up the entirety of their young lives, died on that night of 17 September, 1940.

Kenneth Sparks was thirteen years old, Colin Richardson only eleven on the day when the *City of Benares* left England for Canada with a total complement of 406 – 191 passengers and 215 of a crew. Even today, Kenneth Sparks can recall the dark mutterings of some members of the crew on the choice of a sailing date – Friday the 13th of September.

But no one paid any attention to their gloomy forebodings – certainly none of the children, ranging from five to fifteen years of age, for all of whom this voyage was the most exciting adventure of their lives. There was so much to see – all the other ships in the convoy, the destroyers fussing busily around them, and so much to do – exploring the big liner, playing games, trying their best to do full justice to the magnificent meals set before them.

Nearly all the children were being evacuated, Kenneth Sparks among them, under an official

Government scheme, from heavily bombed areas such as London, Middlesex, Sunderland, Liverpool and Newport: there were nine officially employed escorts to look after them. Colin Richardson was an exception, travelling privately under the care of a Mr Raskay, a Hungarian, who had arranged with Colin's parents to be his guardian for that trip.

On the third day out from England, the destroyers, their charges now safely past the recognized danger zone, turned for home, leaving the convoy on its own. Even among the most hardened sailors in wartime there is always the same feeling of desertion and vulnerability when their naval escort is compelled to withdraw. But this very human apprehension subsided considerably on the evening of the next day when the liner began to pitch and roll in awkward cross-seas as the weather deteriorated and the wind moaned and whistled round the superstructure and through the rigging as it steadily mounted towards gale force, building up the big seas ahead of it.

The tension and the strain aboard the *City of Benares* eased; it was safe now almost to relax. U-boats, of course, were the great menace. But everyone knew how almost impossible it was to launch an accurate torpedo with such seas running, even if a U-boat captain was lucky enough to see them and have time to take an aiming sight, through the cold rain and sleet showers that were beginning to sweep across the darkening sea.

Besides, it was the absolutely recognized convention and law of naval warfare that the torpedoing of liners in gale seas was forbidden: in such heavy seas the chances of survival of the complement of a torpedoed liner were remote indeed.

The *City of Benares* was torpedoed at exactly 10.00 p.m. that night. The torpedo struck the ship far aft on the port side, almost directly opposite the place where the majority of the evacuee children had their quarters. It is not known exactly how many of them lost their lives in that first lethal moment of impact, when the detonating torpedo ripped a huge hole in the unarmoured hull of the *City of Benares* from above to far below the waterline. The probability is that nearly half of these children either died in the first moment, were too dreadfully wounded either to struggle to freedom or even cry out for help, or were trapped in their cabins by warped and buckled doors and taken down with the ship with no one near to help them.

Some children, on the other hand, were at first quite unaware either of the fatal extent of the damage or, indeed, of the fact that there had been any damage at all. Among the unsuspecting ones were Colin Richardson and Kenneth Sparks.

Colin was in his bunk at the time, alone in his cabin, reading a comic. He felt a heavy bump, but paid no attention to it – we can only assume that he found the contents of his comic singularly engrossing – and carried on reading. Not until the alarm bells started ringing did he reluctantly abandon his comic, don a pair of slippers, put on his dressing gown over his pyjamas, his vivid red kapok life jacket – given him by his mother with the instructions that he should wear it always, and of so eye-dazzling a colour that he was already known throughout the ship as Will Scarlet – over his dressing gown, a cork life jacket above that and made his way to the ship's restaurant where he found all the passengers lining up to go to their boat stations.

Kenneth was in bed at 10.00 p.m., and sound asleep. The insistent clamour of the alarm bells brought himself and his two cabin companions – both of whom were to die during the darkness of that night – to their feet, struggling into coats and life jackets before hurrying to their boat positions on the upper deck.

Newly awakened from the soft blanketed warmth of their beds, most of them still half-asleep, the children shivered and tried to crouch more deeply still inside their thin night clothes as the bitter night wind, blowing a full gale now, knifed through their pathetically inadequate garments, drenching them with driving rain and icy hail, blinding them with the bulleting spray whipped off the wave-tops as the already sinking ship, losing way rapidly, began to wallow helplessly in the deep troughs between the seas.

It was not until then that Kenneth Sparks realized what was happening, not until he saw the
blown hatch-covers, the snapped and splintered
mast, the debris lying everywhere, the dazed and
fearful lascar crew members that he understood
that the ship was sinking beneath his feet. Both he
and Colin Richardson remember clearly that there
was no panic, no fear at all among the children,
nothing except the lonely sobbing of one little
boy, crying quietly in the darkness, his voice carrying only faintly in the sudden moments of
silence when the *City of Benares* listed far over to
one side, momentarily blocking the sound and the
power of the gale.

One by one the lifeboats were lowered – a difficult and often dangerous task in a wickedly
rolling, all but stopped ship in those wild and
pitch-dark seas. Some of the lifeboats capsized
immediately, throwing the occupants into the
water – few of these were ever seen again. Some
were swamped and cut adrift. Others came alongside the foot of rope ladders, and women and children clambered down over the side towards them,
as often as not to find that the boats were no
longer there. And then they would find that they
no longer had the strength to climb back up on
deck again: for a few seconds they would hang
there, being battered against the ship's side, alternately being plunged deep into the water or
hauled high above it as the foundering vessel

rolled deeply, sluggishly in the seas: and then their slender strength would fail them, their fingers would open and they were never seen again.

Other women took children in their arms and leapt into the darkness of the sea near a spot where they had seen a raft being dropped over the side. Occasionally – very occasionally – they would reach it, drag themselves aboard and lie there helpless, beaten flat by the wind, the hail and the waves, unable even to so much as raise their heads: more often than not, they would fail to see the raft in the deep gloom of a sea where the towering wave-crests reduced visibility to only a few feet, or, even if they did see one, would find it floating away into the outer darkness more quickly than they could swim after it.

The *City of Benares* sunk in just over ten minutes from the time she was torpedoed, and the wonder of it is that so many managed to get away at all. Miracles of effort and selfless courage were the order of the day. Crew-members leapt into the water to right upturned boats and rescue what passengers they could. Others stayed on the slippery canting decks until the *City of Benares* foundered, struggling to free rafts and jammed lifeboats. All too often they were still struggling when the ship foundered, taking them along with it.

In the minds of nearly every one of the crew and the passengers, the children were the first, last and only thought. The Captain died while still searching for them below decks. So did Colonel Baldwin-Webb, MP for the Wrekin Division of Shropshire, who had acted with imperturbable gallantry throughout and had led many children from the cabins to the lifeboats. So did Colin's guardian, Mr Raskay, who gave up his own place in a lifeboat to a woman and child, turned back, went below, extricated more women and children from blazing cabins, returned to the upper deck and dived into the sea, not to save himself, but to rescue drowning children in the water. It is not known how or where he died, but it was inevitable that he should die. Mr Raskay was a Hungarian, but race and creed meant nothing to him, only humanity.

The chief quartermaster also died in the search for children. He had loaded a lifeboat with women and children, left it in the command of another seaman, climbed back aboard and was never seen again. And the children's official escorts more than lived up to the trust that had been placed in them: only three of them survived.

One of them was Mrs Towns. She stayed to see as many children as possible into the boats, refused a place for herself, and jumped over the side – and she had never swum before in her life. Somehow she reached an upturned boat and clung on to it, one of fifteen, mainly children, who did so. But the cold struck deep, the biting hail and pounding seas numbed arms and bodies and legs, and one by one the children dropped off during that bitter and interminable night. When dawn came, only Mrs Towns and two little girls were left. They survived.

Colin Richardson and Kenneth Sparks were luckier – they managed to get away in lifeboats. Colin remembers vividly the actual moment of the sinking of the *City of Benares*, the spectacle of a man being blasted out through a door crashing back on its hinges, the swift plunge, the bursting open of doors and ventilators as the air pressure inside built up swiftly to an intolerable degree.

He remembers too, the strange sight of the sea dotted with the red lights attached to the life belts of the crew struggling in the water, of those who swam alongside and begged to be taken into the already over-crowded boat; the quiet, unquestioning acceptance of nearly all those who were told there was no room left. They swam away to find what floating debris they could, most of them knowing that it could be only a token postponement of the death by exhaustion and exposure that surely awaited all those without either boat or raft. And the fear-crazed selfishness of one or two who desperately hauled themselves aboard, almost sinking the boat.

'It was a dreadful night,' Colin Richardson remembers. 'Rough and bitterly cold: we were continuously swept by icy wind, rain and sleet.

There was a half-hearted attempt at singing to keep up our spirits – but this did not last long for every time we opened our mouths we got them full of salt water. So we resigned ourselves to concentrating silently and grimly on keeping our place in the boat.'

And, indeed, that was an almost impossible task. Colin's lifeboat was swamped, waterlogged, down to its gunwales in the water and kept afloat only by means of its buoyancy tanks. All were sitting waist-deep – for youngsters like Colin, chest-deep – in the freezing water: every time a wave came along, and they came in endless succession all through that endless night, they had to cling on desperately to prevent themselves from being swept away into the sea: when, like Colin, it was impossible even to reach the floorboards with your feet, the chances of holding on and surviving were negligible. But Colin held on – and he survived.

But many failed to hold on, and many died. One by one they died – from exposure, from just drowning where they sat, from that murderous cramp that weakened their last grip on gunwales and on life and let them be swept over the side to the oblivion and swift release of death by drowning.

The lascar seamen died first – ten of them in swift succession: accustomed all their lives to tropical and subtropical heat, they had no defences against that intolerable cold. Then members of the white crew, and some of the women and children also – up to their chests all night in that freezing water, their hearts just stopped beating. One man went mad and leapt over the side. An old ship's nurse died in Colin's lap after he had spent much time in comforting her, cradling the tired head in his arms, telling her over and over again that the rescue ship was coming. (Mr Richardson, when interviewed recently, did not mention that he had received the King's commendation for bravery for his conduct in the lifeboat that night – surely one of the youngest ever to receive it.)

Dawn came, the sea calmed but the cold was as bitter as ever. Still they died, one by one, but Colin Richardson says his most vivid memory of that day was the sight of an upturned lifeboat with five people clinging to it. 'When first we spotted them, the five waved at us quite happily. But, as the day wore on, one by one they weakened, lost their hold and disappeared. Five, four, three, two, one . . .'

Rescue came at 4.00 p.m. when the destroyer *Hurricane* spotted them and came alongside. Only one person was able to climb up the lowered scrambling nets – 25-year-old Angus MacDonald, the ship's carpenter in charge of the boat, and due to whose magnificent seamanship all the survivors undoubtedly owed their lives. All the survivors . . . ten out of the original forty.

Kenneth Sparks' adventures form a strange contrast to those of Colin Richardson. He too, was in a crowded lifeboat – there were no less than forty-six people in it – but, instead of being eighteen hours in the boat, as Colin was, before being rescued, he and his forty-five companions spent eight days and nights on the surface of the broad and hostile Atlantic – and all forty-six of them miraculously survived.

The difference in survival ratios appears unaccountable at first sight – until it is remembered that Kenneth Sparks' boat did not become swamped and waterlogged, and those in it were not condemned to sit in crouching immobility with the ice-cold water up to their chests: with a judicious sharing out of clothes and covering and huddling together for mutual warmth, even the chill night air of the Atlantic can be borne: it is only when one is immersed in the freezing water itself that there can be no defence.

They also had another great advantage – a means of propulsion through the water. Colin Richardson's lifeboat had had all the oars swept away in the first few moments, but on Kenneth's boat there were no oars to be lost. There was, instead, a screw attached to a long driving shaft, turned by means of vertically mounted push-pull levers between the seats. Not only did this give them directional stability and enable the man in charge, Third Officer Purvis, to keep head to stern on to the worst of the seas, but it also had the great advantage that it could be worked by anyone, the exercise providing life-giving warmth on even the coldest of nights.

They suffered, of course – they suffered cruelly. The cold and exposure were with them all the time – Kenneth spent two months in hospital after his rescue – so were the discomfort and sheer physical fatigue of holding on in the heavy seas. They had food and drink, but not enough: hunger, thirst and sleeplessness were part of their every waking thought. Kenneth Sparks is convinced that he and the five other children aboard that boat owed their survival to Miss Cornish, an official escort later honoured for her courage: she spent nearly all her waking hours in massaging the hands and feet of the children to keep the life-warming blood circulating, giving them exercises and telling them countless stories to keep their minds off their desperate predicament. It says much for the entire success of her efforts when Kenneth says that no one among them ever lost hope of being rescued. And rescued they finally were, located in the first instance by a patrolling plane, and then picked up by a destroyer that took them safely home to Scotland.

Such, then, is the tragic story of the *City of Benares*, surely the most pathetic and heart-rending story of the war at sea. It is reasonable to hope that not even the most ruthless U-boat captain would have torpedoed the *City of Benares* had he known that there were a hundred children aboard, but speculation is no consolation and makes the story no less dreadful.

A dreadful story, but not without its splendour. Apart from Colin and Kenneth and his five companions, only twelve other children survived. A pitiful handful. But it was to give a chance of life to this pitiful handful that dozens of adults out of the 163 crew and passengers gave their own lives willingly and without thought of self.

Who, for instance, was the man who towed a raft away from the sinking ship, just as it was in deadly danger of being sucked under, saw the children on board safely on a lifeboat, turned back again, towed another raft with a woman and four children through the huge seas towards another lifeboat, turned away again into the darkness to search for other survivors and was never seen again?

We do not know, nor does it matter. All we can know is that this man who selflessly gave his own life, would never have thought of recognition nor cared for it had he been given it. An unknown man, a nameless man, but he remains for ever as the symbol of the spirit of the *City of Benares*.

The Gold Watch

His watch was the pride of our captain's life. It was of massive construction, being no less than three inches in diameter; it was made of solid gold; it was beautifully engraved with cabalistic designs of extraordinary intricacy; and finally, it was attached to a chain, whose dimensions, with regard to both length and circumference, had to be seen to be believed. The chain also, needless to say, was made of gold. Anyone, who had the temerity to doubt this last fact, was handed the chain and coldly asked to observe for himself that it was stamped on every link.

In addition to the aforementioned merits, the watch, our captain claimed, was completely moisture-proof. We had, on several occasions, urged him to prove his words by submerging the subject of discussion in a basin of water, but, on each occasion, the captain's reply, uttered in a very injured tone, was to the same effect, namely, that if we did not believe his statement, he was not going to stoop to demonstrate its truth to us. From this, we could only conclude that the captain, like ourselves, had his doubts as to his watch's ability to defy the ravages of water. It was indeed, we knew, a very, very sore point with our captain, one which he longed, with all his heart and soul, to prove, but lacked the courage to put to the final test.

Usually, this watch was hidden from the plebeian gaze – and fingers – in a locked case, which, in its turn, lay in a locked drawer in the captain's cabin. But today, it reposed in the captain's waistcoat pocket, while the chain, such was its length, seemed almost to girdle the area of the captain's maximum circumference. Waistcoats are very uncommon with 'whites', and it was maliciously rumoured that the captain had had his specially made for the purpose of accommodating and displaying the watch and its accessories. Be that as it may, here was our captain, this blistering June afternoon, going ashore for his last interview with his Basrah agents, wearing a genial smile on his face, and, about two feet further south, his beloved time-keeper.

When he came back a bare two hours later, his launch nosing its way through the date-laden lighters surrounding our vessel which was anchored in mid-river, his genial expression was no longer there. Neither was his watch, and our deduction, that the latter circumstance accounted for the former, proved to be correct. Having solicitously helped the red-faced, perspiring captain on board, we waited patiently.

He was, at first, incoherent with rage, and, with his clearly visible, ever-mounting blood pressure, we feared an apoplectic stroke. Fortunately for him, he at last recovered the power of speech, and this undoubtedly relieved, to a great extent, his almost over-powering feelings. He was very bitter. His language, in addition, was shocking, but we had to admit that he had full justification for it.

He had, apparently, been walking peacefully back to the ship from his agents, with malice in his heart towards none, but nevertheless, taking due and proper precautions for the safe-guarding of wallet and watch, when among the riffraff of the street bazaars. Once clear of them, he had dropped these precautions, deeming them need-less, and, at the entrance to the docks, he had had to push his way through a group of Arab sailors, whom he, in his great and regrettable ignorance, had thought to be as honest as himself. (His bit-terness, at this juncture, was truly remarkable.) Suddenly, he had been jostled in the rear with great violence, and, on turning to remonstrate with the discourteous one, had not felt his watch and chain being slipped from their moorings, with that dexterity and efficiency which bespoke of long and arduous practice, so that, when about to resume his journey, he found his watch no longer there.

At this point he again lost the power of speech, and to our fearful and dreading eyes, his entire disintegration appeared not only probable, but imminent. Recovering himself with a masterly effort, however, he resumed his narrative. Although unable to espy the actual perpetrator of the theft, who had, with commendable discretion and alacrity, completely vanished, he had realized that the jostler must have been his confederate, and had pursued the said confederate for over half a mile, before being eluded by the Arab in a crowded thoroughfare. This, we realized, accounted for our captain's complexion and superabundance of perspiration.

Here again, having once more relapsed into incoherency, he was left to his vengeful meditations, alternately muttering 'My watch' and 'The villain', the former with a touching pathos, and the latter, preceded by some highly descriptive adjectives, with an extraordinary depth of feeling.

Thirty hours later found no appreciable diminution in our captain's just and righteous anger, although he could now speak like a rational being, albeit forcefully, concerning his grievous misfortunes of the previous afternoon. We had loaded our last case of dates just on sunset, and, early that morning, even as the first faint streak of grey in the eastern sky heralded the burning day, had gratefully cleared the malodorous port of Basrah.

We were, by this time, fairly into the Gulf and proceeding serenely on our way, South by East, through the stifling tropical night, the darkness of which was but infinitesimally relieved by the cold, unthinkably-distant pinpoints of stars in the moonless night sky.

Our captain, whose outraged feelings evidently refused him the blessed solace of slumber, had recently come up to the bridge, which he was now ceaselessly pacing, very much after the manner of a caged leopard, all the time informing us as to the dire retribution which he intended meting out to the present illegal possessor of his watch, should he ever be fortunate enough to lay hands on him. The lascar quartermaster, very zealous in the captain's presence, was poring over the compass box, while in the bows, the lookout-man was either thinking of his native village in far-off Bombay, or had found sleep vastly easier to come by than our captain.

This last was, of course, pure conjecture, but it must have approximated very closely to the truth, for the first the lookout knew of the dhow lying dead in our path, was when a loud splintering crash, accompanied by even louder frenzied yells, informed him that our steel-bows had smashed the unfortunate dhow to matchwood.

'Don't say we've run down *another* of these b—y dhows,' groaned our captain wearily (it is a surprisingly common occurrence), ringing the engines

down to 'Stop', and bellowing for a boat to be lowered with the utmost expedition. This was done,
and then minutes later the lifeboat returned with
the shivering, brine-soaked crew of the erstwhile
dhow; the captain, duty-bound, went down on
deck to inspect them, as they came on board.

The rope ladder twitched, and as the first luckless
victim – how luckless, he did not then completely
realize – appeared over the side, the captain's jaw
dropped fully two inches, and he stood as if trans-
fixed.

'That's the gentleman I chased yesterday' – he
ejaculated joyfully ('gentleman', as will be readily
understood, is employed euphemistically), then
stopped, staring, with rapidly glazing eyes, at the
second apparition, who had just then topped the
railing. Dependent from this, the second, 'gentleman's' undeniably filthy neck, and reaching to his
waist, was a most unusual ornament for an
impoverished Arab – no less an object than our
captain's purloined watch and chain, thus miraculously restored to him, by the playful caprices of
Fortune.

With drawn breath, and with sincere pity in our
hearts, we waited for the heavens to fall, for the
captain to execute his oft-repeated, bloodthirsty
promises, for, in short, the instant and complete
annihilation of the Arabs (four in all), who were
regarding the captain with the utmost trepidation,
which they were at no pains to conceal.

To our no small astonishment – and, it may be added, relief – the expected Arab-massacre failed to materialize. Instead, stepping quietly forward and lovingly removing his watch and chain from the neck of the cringing, violently-shivering Arab, the captain, in a strangely gentle tone, in which there seemed, to us, to be a barely repressed inflection of triumph, merely said, 'Take these men below and give them something warm to eat; we'll hand them over to the Bahrein police, in the morning.'

We were astounded. We were amazed. We were utterly and completely dumbfounded. Our modest comprehension could not grasp it. What, we asked ourselves, wonderingly, was the reason for this incredible change of front? We were not left long in ignorance.

Swinging round on us, and brandishing his watch on high, the captain shouted: 'See! – er, I mean, hear!' We heard. The clamorous ticktock, ticktock of his watch would have put any self-respecting alarm clock to shame.

'Waterproof!' he cried exultingly. 'Waterproof, you blasted unbelievers! Waterproof!'

It was, I verily believe, the supreme moment of our captain's life.

Rendezvous

It was quite dark now and the Great North Road, the A1, that loneliest of Europe's highways, almost deserted. At rare intervals, a giant British Roadways truck loomed out of the darkness: a courteous dipping of headlamps, immaculate hand-signals, a sudden flash of sound from the labouring diesel – and the A1 was lonelier than ever. Then there was only the soothing hum of tyres, the black ribbon of highway, and the headlights of the Jaguar, weirdly hypnotic, swathing through the blackness.

Loneliness and sleep, sleep and loneliness. The enemies, the co-drivers of the man at the wheel; the one lending that extra half pound of pressure to the accelerator, the other, immobile and ever-watchful, waiting his chance to slide in behind the wheel and take over. I knew them well and I feared them.

But they were not riding with me tonight. There was no room for them. Not with so many passengers. Not with Stella sitting there beside me, Stella of the laughing eyes and sad heart, who had died in a German concentration camp. Not with Nicky, the golden boy, lounging in the back seat, or Passière, who had never returned to his sun-drenched vineyards in Sisteron. No room for sleep and loneliness? Why, by the time you had crowded in Taffy the engineer, complaining as bitterly as ever and Vice-Admiral Starr and his bushy eyebrows, there was hardly room for myself.

I glanced at the dashboard clock. 2.00 a.m. Nine hours since I had left Inverness and only one stop for gas. I realized I was very hungry.

A couple of miles further on a neon sign blinked garishly through the heavy drizzle. A drivers' pull-up. I swung the Jaguar off the road, parked beside the heavy trucks and limped inside.

It was a bright, noisy, cheerful place, about half full. I picked up my bacon, sausages and eggs and went over to an empty table by the window.

The meal finished, I lit a cigarette and stared out unseeingly into the driving rain. Now and again I could hear the rumble and swish as a truck or night-coach rolled by on the Great North Road.

The Great North Road. The prelude, the curtain call to all the highlights of my life – long Italian summers on my father's ship, Oxford and the Law, the Royal Naval Barracks, Portsmouth. All these other times, I reflected, there had been uncertainty.

So, too, this time. All these other times excitement, anticipation. But this time only doubt and wonder, foreboding and slow anger.

I fished out Nicky's telegram again

ONLY THE GOOD DIE YOUNG STOP HALLELUJAH STOP THE DE'IL LOOKS AFTER HIS AIN STOP NOW SUCCESSFUL BREEDER OF OIL WELLS STOP STAYING SAVOY WITH ALL THE OTHER MILLIONAIRES STOP RRR

NICKY

I pushed the telegram back into my pocket. RRR. The Special Service code-sign – 'Where do we rendezvous?' I had wired back SEE YOU SAVOY 7 P.M. WEDNESDAY.

Even now I did not know why I had done it. It just had to be done. This was one loose end in my life that simply had to be cut off. Courage, fear, curiosity, anger – these did not enter into it. There was just simple compulsion. This I had to do.

I paid my check, climbed into the Jaguar, pulled out on the A1, set the hand throttle and headed south.

I was confused. The bit about the De'il – the Devil looks after his own – a phrase he had picked up from me: that I could understand. He had seen the flaming eruption of disintegrating steel and burning oil as the Heinkel's glider-bomb had smacked accurately into the engine room of the F149. I had no right to be alive, the surgeon had said – but he had made a pretty good job of my crocked leg and mangled arm.

But I couldn't figure the rest of the telegram. It was too friendly. Too friendly by half for a man who, when we had last parted – five minutes before the explosion – had been standing on a desolate Tuscan beach at the wrong end of my Service Colt .45. I could see him yet, could see the anger dying in his eyes, the disbelief, the astonishment, the emotionless mask. I had stood there trying to hate him – and failing miserably – and trying not to hate myself. I had failed in that too. And I heard again his promise, quiet, almost conversational: 'Don't forget, Mac – I'll be looking you up one of these days.'

I sighed. Our first meeting had been rather different. I flicked the dashboard switch. 2.45. Two hundred miles to London. I shoved the hand throttle up a notch.

Malta, 1943. The George Cross island. The island of Faith, Hope and Charity – the three obsolete fighters pitted against the savagery of the Axis air fleets. Malta. The sorely battered capital of Valetta and the Grand Harbour, that destination of a very few, very lucky merchant ships, of the 40-knot plus gauntlet-running minelaying cruisers, of the submarine gasoline tankers, of the immortal 'Ohio'.

But the war was very far away that Spring morning. All was peaceful and still and bathed in sunshine as I walked into the Admiralty HQ.

'Lieutenant McIndoe to see Admiral Starr?' the duty petty officer repeated. 'Along the passage, first on the left, sir. He's alone just now.'

I knocked and went in. A large bare room, with Venetian blinds and walls covered with maps, it was completely dominated by the huge figure sitting behind the only table in the room. Two hundred and fifty pounds if an ounce, red-faced, white-haired and with bushy eyebrows, Vice-Admiral Starr had become a legend in his own lifetime. He had the face and expression of a bucolic farmer, a mind like a rapier and a deep-rooted intolerance of those who wasted either time or speech.

He pushed some papers away in a folder and motioned me to a seat.

"Morning, McIndoe. Carried out your instructions?' he asked.

'To the letter, sir,' I replied carefully. 'Gunboat F149 is completely stripped. The extra fuel tanks are fitted and the short- and long-range receiving and transmitting sets were installed yesterday. She's fuelled, provisioned and ready for sea.'

He nodded in satisfaction. 'And your crew?'

'The best, sir. Experienced, completely reliable.'

'Right.' He stood up. 'You'll contact Ravallo this evening and receive final instructions from him.'

'Ravallo, sir?'

'Major Ravallo, US Army. A top espionage agent and just about the best lend-lease bargain ever. From now on, he's your immediate boss.'

I felt distinctly aggrieved. 'Am I to understand, sir –'

'These are your orders,' he interrupted flatly. 'Besides,' he chuckled, 'Ravallo will welcome you with open arms. The last time he came back from Sicily, he had to swim the last two miles. Damned annoyed, he was.'

'Quite so, sir. Do I meet Ravallo here?'

Admiral Starr coughed. 'Well, no, not exactly. Major Ravallo is an American – ' he spoke as if this explained everything – 'and not subject to our discipline. You'll find him in the Triannon bar at six o'clock.'

'Have another, Mac,' Nicky Ravallo urged hospitably. 'You'll be needing it tonight yet.'

Major Ravallo, I reflected, would have made a big hit in Hollywood. With his dark, tousled hair, crinkling blue eyes, dark tan, white teeth and weird hodgepodge of a uniform designed strictly by himself, he looked ready-made material for a Caribbean pirate or a second d'Artagnan. But the gallant Major, it seemed to me, treated war much too lightly; besides, I was still smarting from the insult of being placed under an American's command – and from his smiling refusal to give me any details of that night's operation until we got to sea.

'No thanks,' I replied stiffly. 'So far I've never felt the need for any pre-operational stoking up

on alcohol. And I'm not starting now.' I knew I
was behaving badly.

'Suit yourself, Scotty.' Ravallo was not only
unruffled but positively affable. 'Starr tells me
you're a specialist on the Italian coast and language and just about the best gunboat handler in
the business. That's all I want. Come along.'

In silence we walked through the white-walled
streets towards the harbour and in silence we
descended by the fearsome open elevator on the
cliff-face to the gathering gloom of Christ's steps.
Here we hired a dico and were rowed out to
Motor Gunboat F149, moored at the far end of
Angelo creek.

Once aboard, I had him meet my crew – Taffy,
Passière, Hillyard, Johnson, Higgins and Wilson,
my second in command. They seemed favourably
impressed by Ravallo, and he by them, although I
did not take too kindly to his cheerful invitation to
'just call me Nicky, boys.' They would be calling
me 'Sammy' next and I wasn't sure that I would
like that.

'How come Passière?' Ravallo asked when we
were alone again. 'Hardly an Anglo-Saxon name
that.'

'Like Ravallo?' I suggested.

He laughed. '*Touchè*. But still,' he persisted,
'what's he doing here?'

'Free French,' I explained. 'There are thousands
of them on our side – mostly in their own ships.

He's a refugee from Vichy France, a holder of the *Croix de Guerre* and just about the best radio operator I've ever known. I hope,' I added sweetly, 'that you have no objections to the presence of non-British nationals aboard this boat?'

'Sorry again,' he laughed. 'I guess I asked for that.' He ran his hand ruefully through his thick black hair and grinned quizzically at me.

For the first time, I smiled back.

An hour later, the 149 cleared the entrance of Grand Harbour. Ravallo was in the wheelhouse with me, sitting on a camp-stool, quietly smoking.

He spoke suddenly.

'We're going to Sicily, Mac. Rendezvous, midnight, two miles north-west of Cape Passero. OK?'

I said nothing, but turned to my charts and tables.

'Half-speed, Chief,' I said to Wilson. 'Course zero-five-zero. Hillyard, Johnson on watch. Right?'

'Aye, aye, sir.'

Ravallo jumped to his feet.

'Here, what's this?' he demanded swiftly. 'Half-speed? Look, Mac, we gotta hit the rendezvous on the nose. Midnight, Scotty, midnight – not tomorrow morning. Last time I came from Sicily it took fourteen hours. Including two hours swimming,' he added bitterly.

Wilson and I grinned at each other.

'Chief,' I said sorrowfully, 'I'm afraid we've a doubter on our hands. The Major and I are taking a walk forrard. Ask Taffy to open her up – demonstration purposes only.'

The demonstration was brief and entirely effective. At its conclusion we walked slowly aft to the stern and sat down, leaning against the recently emptied depth-charge racks, Ravallo looking very thoughtful, almost dazed.

The effect was almost always the same. The hypnotic effect of the rushing waters and the gigantic bow-wave, coupled with the sheer physical shock of the bone-jarring vibrations of the deck and the banshee clamour of the great aero-engines was almost literally stunning.

Ravallo broke the silence.

'Sorry again, Mac.' His face lit up with remembered enthusiasm. 'My God, Mac, that must be one of the last thrills left on earth. What was she doing – forty-five, fifty knots?'

'Official secret,' I said solemnly. 'Seriously, though, I don't think you need worry about anything on the surface of the Mede catching us. And now – how about some more information, Major?'

'Nicky,' he corrected absently. 'Right, Mac, this is how it is.

'This cloak-and-dagger sealed orders act isn't just for fun. It's a must. Do you know how many agents we've lost this year in Italy?' he asked slowly. 'Twenty-six.' He pounded his fist, very gently, on the deck, his eyes quiet, his voice level.

'Twenty-six,' I echoed. 'That's impossible.' (Neither of us knew at the time that the British had already lost twice that number in Holland alone. All died.)

He didn't seem to hear me.

'A couple by natural hazards,' he went on. 'Maybe half-a-dozen through leaks. The rest – ' he waved a hand forrard – 'well, that's what this boat is for.' He paused.

'Well, go on.' I was becoming interested.

'German and Italian radio monitoring stations,' he explained. 'Almost all information is sent out by radio. Fairly powerful transmitting sets which are as easily picked up by the enemy as by us. A few cross-bearings and – finish.'

'But you still haven't explained – '

'I'm coming to that. The idea is to fit our agents with weak, short-range transmitters – hardly more than fields – which cuts out ninety per cent of the risk of detection. Your boat will lie close off-shore – two or three miles – pick up our agents' reports on its short-range receiver and re-transmit to base by the big RCA. Starr says he will have six of these boats in action by the end of the year.'

'Aha!' I said. 'Light dawns. I should have thought of that before. It should work.'

'It *must* work,' he said heavily. 'We've lost too many of our best agents already.'

We sat on deck for several minutes, companionably silent, having the last smoke on deck of the day. Presently Ravallo spun his cigarette over the side and rose easily to his feet.

'Mac?'

I turned my head.

'Do you mind if I have a look at the radio room?'

'Help yourself. Passière's having supper just now.'

He left me. I sat for another couple of minutes, pondering over Ravallo's news, then went to darken ship.

After supper, we went to the wheelhouse. I took over from Wilson, who went below. The sea was as calm as a mill-pond and there was no moon that night. Conditions were ideal.

I looked at my watch. 11.00 p.m. I wished I could smoke.

'What happens at the rendezvous, Nicky?' I asked.

'Picking up an agent,' he said briefly. 'The Syracuse area is getting too hot these days.'

'Friend of yours?'

'Sort of. One can't afford to have friends in our line,' he said quietly. 'Too much grief. Besides – ' he paused – 'Stella doesn't encourage – er – friendship.'

'Stella?' I glanced quickly at him. 'You mean – '

'Yeah, he's a she.' Nicky was laconic. 'Why not? She's one of the best in the business – and less liable to suspicion. Parachuted in two months ago.'

I turned this over on my mind.

'Speaks the language fluently, I suppose?'

'Strange if she didn't,' Nicky smiled. 'She was born in Leghorn.'

'An Italian!' I made a grimace of distaste. 'Well, I suppose the money's good.'

In two quick strides he was beside me, his hand gripping my shoulder.

'Watch it, Scotty,' he murmured softly. 'Careful of what you say. She's a naturalized American, same as I am.'

Silently I cursed myself and gently disengaged his hand.

'Looks as if this is going to be a record night for apologies, Nicky,' I said wryly. 'Damned stupid of me. Keep your eyes skinned, will you?'

We spent an hour of steadily mounting anxiety waiting at the rendezvous. Nicky, I could see, was worried and upset – not at all in character, I thought.

Shortly after one o'clock we heard the angry hum of a small outboard. A 12-foot skiff with two dark figures aboard appeared out of the darkness and slid smoothly alongside. A bump, a couple of out-stretched arms, a heave – just so quickly was the small boat away again and a slender figure in slacks and windbreaker standing there on deck, shivering involuntarily in the cold.

Nicky's voice was harsh and low. Perhaps from relief, perhaps from anger.

'You're late. Far too damn late. How often do you have to be told not to keep a boat waiting in enemy waters? Had to powder your pretty little nose, I suppose?'

'Sorry, Nicky,' she pleaded. Her voice was warm and soft and husky. 'Johnny found a leak in the petrol tank and had to return for more and –'

'Keep quiet!' I whispered urgently.

Nicky spoke angrily: 'Look, Mac, that's the second time – '

'Shut up and listen!'

This time they, too, heard it – a muffled creak, ominous, stealthy.

'Petrol, hell!' I said softly, bitterly. 'Nipped back to give his pals the tip-off, you mean. Take her to my cabin, Nicky, quickly.'

She broke from his grip and caught my lapel.

'Get away as fast as you can,' she whispered. 'The Germans have two fast motor-launches in harbour. They're armed. They're manned day and night and – '

'Take her below,' I interrupted. I wrenched her hand away. 'And keep her there.'

The crew of the 149 were superbly trained. A couple of low-voiced commands and, as our port and starboard magnesium rockets curved upwards, the 149 was already thrusting through the water at close on twenty knots. Wilson was behind the searchlight and every gun was manned.

There were three of them astern of us, cockle-shell rowing boats, with three soldiers – Germans, I thought – in each, every one life-jacketed and armed to the teeth – as wicked looking a boarding party as I'd seen for a long time. But this was going to be easy.

I stopped the engine momentarily, wound down a window, yelled to the crew to get under cover, called to Taffy for full speed and swung the 149 round in a skidding half-turn.

Twenty seconds later it was all over. A brief fusillade of carbine shots – some starring the wheelhouse's bullet-proof windows – a couple of twenty-five knot racing turns and the three boats were swamped and overturned. We stopped, fished a couple of bedraggled soldiers from the water – prisoners were always welcome at HQ – and headed south-west for home.

Not till then did I realize that Nicky and Stella were with me in the wheelhouse.

'I thought I told you to get below,' I said angrily.

'No fear!' said Nicky enthusiastically. 'That was too good to miss.'

'Please do as I ask. You're only in the way here,' I said coldly. 'Higgins will bring you coffee and sandwiches.'

When I joined them half an hour later, the coffee and sandwiches were still untouched. Stella was sitting on my bunk. This was the first time I had seen her face and not even the harsh glare of the deckhead light could mar the flawless beauty of its perfect oval, the olive complexion, the patrician little nose, the plaited coils of hair, lustrous and silky, black as a raven's wing. Not even her swimming eyes and tear-smudged cheeks could do that.

'Oh Lord!' I said tiredly. 'What's up now?'

'Professional disagreement,' Nicky said shortly. His black hair was more tousled than ever. 'Look, Mac, there's been a slip-up somewhere. A leak from base is almost impossible. So it must have been Stella. Somewhere, somehow, in the past day or two, she made a mistake. She must have.'

'But I didn't, Nicky,' she whispered huskily. 'I swear I didn't. I didn't put a foot wrong. Honestly, Nicky.'

He looked – and sounded – pretty weary.

'OK, OK, Stella. Let's leave it at that.'

Nicky and I went outside and stood leaning on the rail. After a minute I turned to him.

'Nicky.'

'Yeah?'

'You don't seriously suspect her, do you?'

He turned slowly and looked at me.

'Just how damned stupid can you get, Scotty?' he asked. His voice was cold, hostile. Abruptly, he turned and left me.

I was alone with my thoughts. I had plenty to think about.

* * *

'What do you reckon Admiral Starr made of it all?' Nicky asked.

I finished off my Benedictine, put my glass down thoughtfully and smiled at him. Eight hours' sleep had put us both in an infinitely better humour.

'Difficult to say. He's a cagey old bird. Personally, I think he's as much in the dark as we are.'

'Just about what I figured. Hullo, here's Stella.'

He nodded towards the street door of the Triannon and waved.

She was worth waving at, I thought soberly. Dressed in a plain button-through white frock, quite uncluttered by any jewellery, she looked, and was, a lovely and desirable girl.

Nicky must have been watching my face.

'She's quite something, isn't she, Mac?'

I nodded slowly, but said nothing.

'Couldn't blame anyone for falling for her,' he murmured. The smile on his face was half a question. 'Even you, Mac.'

'I might at that,' I replied quietly.

He looked at me, a curious, enigmatic expression on his face.

'Don't, laddie, don't.' He grinned. 'It's like I told you, Mac – in our line of business, it's just too much grief. 'Evening, Stella.' He smiled at her and turned towards the barman. 'A Dubonnet for the lady.'

Conversation was desultory for a few minutes. I lit a cigarette, peered into the bar mirror and said suddenly: 'You two made your peace yet?'

Stella smiled. 'Yes.'

'I thought so.' I reached round her and firmly disengaged the hand which I had seen in the mirror gently closing over Stella's.

'Ah, ah, Major Ravallo!' I said severely. 'Don't touch! Not in our line of business – too much grief, you know.'

They looked at each other, then at me, and laughed.

I felt suddenly tired. Not sleepy – just tired. The rain had stopped and a moon was struggling to break through the watery clouds. The facia clock stood at 4.15. Another one hundred miles to London.

It was the first and last meeting with Nicky, I reflected, that was etched so clearly in my mind. The years between, in hazy retrospect, were a kaleidoscopic blur.

We three – Stella, Nicky and I – had grown very close to each other. With the crew of the 149, we had been a great team – at first. Three times our base of operation had shifted – Palermo, Salerno, Naples. Eleven times we had set them down, singly or together, on the enemy coast, and each time picked them up without mishap. The completely selfless devotion to their job of my crew – especially Wilson and Passière, both of whom had twice refused promotion – was extraordinary.

But, towards the end, there had been a steady deterioration – in several ways. Laughter, I could see, came less and less readily to Stella's eyes. She had grown thinner, was intense at times, at others listless and despondent. Scarcely a week went by but she saw Forts, Liberators and Lancasters battering targets in her own homeland – twice, to my certain knowledge, on information supplied by herself. It must have been hell for her.

Nicky, too, had changed. The laughing cavalier of the Malta days had vanished. Taciturn and uncommunicative, he rarely smiled. It was his homeland too, of course. Perhaps it was Stella, but I was pretty sure it wasn't. Nicky, after his one brief lapse in Malta, followed his own example and armoured himself in indifference towards her. They rarely spoke together without bickering.

Again, in the winter of '43, a mixed battalion of Rangers and Commandos, leapfrogging the Allied Army, had landed on the coast in a quiet bay selected by HQ and guaranteed clear by Nicky and Stella. Half-an-hour after the last man had gone ashore, the battalion had been cut to pieces by a Panzer division. It could have been coincidence.

A month later, the largest arms and ammunition drop of the war had fallen into German hands. The waiting Partisans had been wiped out – completely. That, too, could have been coincidence – but coincidence couldn't explain how the enemy had obtained the correct recognition signals and the agreed sequence of flare markers.

Finally, in the late Spring, eight agents had been set down near Civitavecchia by the 149. For three nights we had waited for radio signals. None came. We did not need to ask what had happened.

It was growing light now on the A1, but there was no corresponding lift in my spirits. I felt again that same nameless sadness, that same heaviness of heart I had felt on that blazing summer afternoon as I had made my way to Admiral Starr's office in Naples. I had known, subconsciously at least, why he had sent for me.

Admiral Starr, too, had changed. He was tireder now, his face more lined. And he was brutally frank.

'"Betrayal" is a nasty word, McIndoe,' he said heavily. 'The time has come to use it. Thousands of British and American boys are being maimed and killed every month. Kid gloves are out. Agreed?'

I nodded silently.

'We have no proof,' he went on bitterly. 'Not a scrap. But this I do know. Three coincidences are just three to many. Also, after that battalion massacre, the base security staff was completely changed. It made no difference. The leakage is at your end, McIndoe. The logic of it is simple.' He paused, and smiled thinly. 'I asssume I am above suspicion.'

He looked down at his hands.

'Ravallo and his friend are both Italian-Americans,' he went on quietly. 'US Army Intelligence swears both are absolutely loyal. I'm not so sure. Neither, I suspect, are you, McIndoe.'

He glanced at me under his bushy eyebrows – to see how I was taking it, I suppose. Again I said nothing.

'You will meet them in Anzio tomorrow,' he continued harshly. 'You will tell them that, owing to a base HQ leak, this will be their last mission. You will lead them to believe that this is a normal mission organized by our base security staff. This is untrue. Only you and I, McIndoe, know of this. Both will be allowed to come and go as they wish until they embark on the 149. Understand?'

'Yes, sir.'

'Can you trust your chief and radio man?'

'Implicitly, sir.'

'Good. You will take them and them alone into your confidence. Inadvisable, perhaps, but unavoidable. They are to deny all access to deck signalling equipment and the radio room. Any questions?'

I didn't reply at once. The word 'radio room' had exploded a bomb in my mind. And when they came down, the pieces were all in place. I cursed myself for my own stupidity.

'No questions, sir.' I took a deep breath. This was going to hurt. 'As you infer, sir, I have had my suspicions for some time. It's Ravallo, sir.'

He looked up sharply. 'Good God, man, how can you be so sure?'

I told him.

We left Naples at dawn and arrived in Anzio at midday. On the way I had briefed both Wilson and Passière. They were incredulous, of course, and grieved – there was no other word for it. They had developed an affection for Nicky and Stella almost as deep as mine.

At midnight that night the 149 was lying offshore three miles north of Civitavecchia. Both Ravallo and Stella were very quiet – had been ever since I had told them. On the whole, they seemed relieved.

Only Stella was to go ashore. She was to contact the local Partisan group – who had already been warned by Starr, by parachute drop the previous night, to prepare for a German sortie tonight – and radio back as soon as possible. I had expected Ravallo to protest violently when Starr's radio instructions to that effect had come through a couple of hours ago – but he had said nothing.

His easy acceptance of the orders confirmed me in my suspicions. I guessed this suited him perfectly. I suspected he had contacted the enemy before leaving Anzio. How, I didn't know – but the place was reported to be swarming with spies. Ravallo certainly hadn't had a chance to communicate with anyone ashore since embarking on the 149. Wilson and Passière had seen to that.

Stella went ashore and Hillyard rowed the dinghy back. Three hours later the radio room receiver started crackling. Ravallo and I stood just inside the radio room door, waiting.

Suddenly Passière's expression changed. He looked startled, apprehensive. He listened intently, jabbed furiously three or four times at the transmitting key, then leapt to his feet, tearing his headphones off. His hands were shaking.

They've got her!' he burst out. 'They've got Stella! Just after the code-sign and acknowledgement came *MMR, MMR'* (the Special Service code-sign for danger). 'Then something about an armoured car. Then – finish.' He cut down his right arm in a gesture of finality.

I felt sick inside. The best laid plans of mice and men . . . There had been a slip-up somewhere. Stella – captured! Why hadn't the Partisans been there?

I flung a glance at Ravallo. His face was expressionless. I wondered savagely how he ought to look. Was that the way Judas had looked? Was Nicky Ravallo paid in pieces of silver?

I wrenched myself back into the present. I knew then what I would have to do. I also knew what it would mean for me – court martial. Just then I didn't care.

Swiftly I turned to Ravallo.

'Do you know where she went, Nicky?' I demanded.

'Sure I do.' He had divined my intentions immediately and was into the boat before me.

Hillyard rowed us ashore. We jumped out on the pebbly shore and raced up the beach. Halfway up I stopped short and called softly.

'Nicky!'

He turned round.

'Dammit, Scotty, there's no time – '

He broke off short. His eyes didn't have to be very good to see the dull gleam of the .45 in my hand.

He remained motionless.

'What is this?' he asked slowly.

'This,' I said, 'is as far as I go. Incidentally, that was a marvellous piece of acting. Congratulations.'

He was a trier, I had to admit. The anger, the impatience, the puzzlement – they were perfectly done.

'Stay where you are!' I said sharply. He had taken a step forward.

'The only explanation you are entitled to is why you are still alive. I'll tell you.

'Renegades, Ravallo, aren't always monsters. I liked you, Ravallo – in your own idiom, I thought you were one helluva good guy. Secondly, war is no reason for inhumanity. You know that. And I think it inhuman to ask a man to spy on his own country.'

'What are you trying to tell me?' His voice was almost a whisper.

'Save it, Ravallo. I could have had you taken back to Naples,' I went on. 'You know what that

means. Court martial – and the firing squad. Or
you could have been dropped over the side. I drew
the line at that also. So,' I added, 'you're getting
what you never gave Stella, Ravallo – a chance.
Among your own people,' I finished bitterly.

'You betrayed yourself a year ago, Ravallo. I
didn't get it till yesterday. Remember Passero?
Remember the rowing boats the Germans used
that night to try to board us? Remember the visit
you paid to the empty radio room? Remember the
fast launches that Stella said the Germans had in
Passero? Remember, Ravallo, remember?'

I flung the words at him, hammered them at
him. They had no effect. He seemed dazed,
showed no reaction at all. The man was a superb
actor.

'How were the Germans tipped off, Ravallo?' I
went on relentlessly. 'Why didn't they send their
fast launches after us? I'll tell you, Ravallo.
Because they knew they hadn't a hope in hell of
catching us. They knew that a sneak attack was
their only hope. They knew that because *you* told
them, Ravallo. And *only* you could have told
them. Only *you* of all suspects fulfilled the four
essential conditions – you knew the speed of the
149, you knew our destination that night, you
knew how to use and had access to a transmitter –
the I49's.'

There was no answer to this and Ravallo knew
it. There could be no defence – only denial. He

said nothing for a long time. His head was bent. The moon, almost full, had broken through the cloud, and I was in a hurry to be gone.

He lifted his head slowly and looked at me.

'Got it all buttoned up, haven't you, Mac?'

'I have indeed. I wish to God I hadn't. You gave yourself away again today.

'Starr had it narrowed down to you two – you and Stella. He guessed it was you – rather, I did. He had fixed it so as to give you a chance to sell Stella down the river. You thought her usefulness was over. So you sold her down the river. You didn't know that base weren't briefed on this mission, Ravallo, did you? Only you, Stella, Starr and I knew. And once, Ravallo, I could have sworn you loved that girl.' I looked at him, trying hard to hate him. 'You know,' I said, 'I couldn't have done that to a dog.'

His face was expressionless.

'So you threw her to the wolves? Is that it, Mac?'

Why hadn't the Partisans looked after her, I thought to myself. They had plenty of warning. Illogically, I felt guilty as hell and knew for the first time the salt taste of self-loathing. But I didn't show it – I knew that.

'I had my orders. Besides, Nicky,' I added ironically, 'we should never have succeeded without your invaluable cooperation. Goodbye.'

He called after me. 'Mac!'

I turned round.

'Don't forget, Mac, I'll be looking you up one of these days.'

One of these days. Well, that was it.

I had arrived in London at 6.00 a.m. and gone straight to bed. For hours I had lain awake, trying to figure the whole thing out.

It was a mess and it was fantastic. Why hadn't the Allied authorities seized him after the war? He was obviously a prosperous man now. He had much to lose – I marvelled at his nerve in seeking me out.

What did he want, I wondered. Just to gloat? No, whatever he was, Ravallo had never been small-minded. Revenge – it could only be that. But how? A fusillade of shots in the lounge of the Savoy? Ridiculous – just too fantastic. Besides, Nicky was a smart boy. About midday I gave the whole thing up and fell into a troubled sleep.

7.00 p.m. The lounge at the Savoy was full, but I saw him almost at once. It wasn't difficult. He was the only man in the place wearing a lounge suit. He was over by the far wall and, characteristically, had managed to obtain – and retain – a table for himself.

There was no change in Ravallo that I could see. Still the same vital, dark haired, laughing d'Artagnan – and he was laughing now. Laughing – the smile on the face of the tiger.

He leapt from his table and came swiftly towards me, hand outstretched, his white teeth shining in a great grin of welcome.

'Mac, you old son of a gun!' he shouted cheerfully. 'Man, oh man, but it's good to see you again!'

'Meaning you'd lost all hope of ever catching up with me?' I asked quietly. I made no move to take his hand and he let it drop slowly to his side. I was dimly aware that dozens of curious people were looking at us.

Ravallo still smiled – albeit a trifle ruefully now. It was the perfect picture of the unjustly slighted friend, still good humoured and tolerant. You're good, Ravallo, I thought, you're damned good.

'My address,' I said harshly. 'How did you get it?'

'Easy. The Admiralty – you're still on the Reserved List.' The smile was a trifle uncertain now.

I should have thought of that.

'Well, I'm here now. What's on the cards, Ravallo? A cosy little Italian knifing session? Maybe one of your pals in the Mafia? What do you want, Ravallo?'

'Civility, Scotty, civility.' The smile was quite gone now. 'And five minutes of your time – if you can stop being completely daft for that length of time. Here's my table. How about a drink?'

'The lapse of nine years and the fact that the war is over doesn't make treason any less heinous a crime.' I didn't bother to lower my voice. 'As for the drink, not with you, Ravallo. I'll get my own.'

Something was badly out of focus – I needed time to think. I turned to push my way to the bar through the knot of people crowding round.

Ravallo caught my arm. He was immensely strong.

'Same as Civitavecchia, eh, Mac?' he asked softly. 'Still the same jury, judge and executioner. Is that it?'

'Yes,' I said evenly. 'That's it.'

'And I'm the condemned man?'

'You're the condemned man.'

'A last favour, then.' His voice was very low. 'It's my privilege.'

Something about him, about his voice, his eyes, his desperate sincerity caught me. Not even Spencer Tracy was that good. For the first time I knew doubt.

I followed him slowly back to his table and sat down. The curious crowd gradually melted away.

'Well, I'm listening.'

'You don't even have to do that, Mac,' he said smilingly. 'Just read these.'

Carefully he placed two documents on the table and smoothed them out. After some hesitation, I picked one up.

It was a transcript from the US Navy Records Office. It had been made in the Pentagon and ran as follows:

Leading Signalman Georges Passière, Official No P/JX 282131.

A body, dressed in Royal Naval tropical kit, was found on the beach, fourteen miles South of Civitavecchia. 16 May, 1944.

Identified as above rating by identity disc.

Secret lining discovered in flap of belt pouch. Oilskin envelope. List of thirty transmitting and receiving station wavelengths: VHF (very high frequency): mainly short-range. Six positively identified as German: remainder unknown.

Slowly, ever so slowly, I laid the document on the table. I was dimly aware of a waiter by my side, and a tray of glasses. Automatically, unseeingly almost, I picked up a glass with one hand, the remaining document with the other.

Deutscher Geheimdienst.

German Counter-Intelligence Records captured Turin.

Decoded Naples, October 1944.

Luigi Metastasio: Born Rome 1919.

(Then followed an account of Metastasio's school life, civilian employment, Fascist indoctrination, army service, counter-intelligence training.) Speaks French, German and English fluently: smuggled into France April 1940, German-occupied France August 1940, thence to Fecamp: fishing boat to England. Accepted Portsmouth barracks May, 1941: qualified telegraphist.

The rest was unimportant – and I knew the last line before I read it.

Assumed name – Georges Passière.

I placed this report on the other and gazed at it as though hypnotized. I said nothing – I couldn't say anything. Neither thoughts nor words would come. My mind seemed to have stopped. I felt beaten, empty, sick – and hopelessly confused.

Nicky was merciful, infinitely so. I hardly heard his voice at first.

'It was a sweet racket, Mac. The beauty of the short-range receiver.' He laughed shortly. 'Sure the Germans couldn't monitor our agents' radio messages. By the same paradigm we couldn't monitor Passière's short-range reports, probably relayed back immediately afterwards to German and Italian listening posts. The massacred Partisans, the butchery of the Rangers and the Commandos, the capture of our agents, the tip-off at Passero – all friend Passière's work.'

'And – and Stella?' With a great effort I forced the words out. My mind was working again and the realization, stark and unforgiving, of what I had done these long years ago now smashed home like a hammer blow.

I answered my own question, my voice an unbelieving whisper.

'Passière! That's how Stella went, Nicky. It must have been. Passière! I, *I* took Passière into my confidence. Nicky – *I told him everything*!'

'Yeah,' murmured Nicky quietly. I thought it had to be something like that. If he knew she was finished, no more use to him, he would try to tip them off, wouldn't he?'

Maybe Nicky didn't stop there. Maybe he went on talking. I don't know. All I know is that his voice, quiet and level and kind, died away in my ear. I couldn't hear Nicky any longer. I couldn't even look at him. I knew I should be apologizing, saying something about never forgiving myself – but I knew that this lay outwith the reach of words.

'*I* sold her down the river. I threw her to the wolves,' I said dully. '*I* did that. Nobody else, Nicky, only me. Just me.' I buried my head in my hands.

I knew a hundred pairs of eyes were on me and I didn't care. The lounge had gone very quiet. The seconds – each one an eternity of self-loathing, of bitterness, of despair – ticked slowly by. Slowly, terribly slowly.

Suddenly, petrifyingly, a pair of soft hands clasped gently over my eyes and a well-remembered voice, husky with emotion, whispered compassionately:

'Enough is enough, Nicky. Hullo, Mac, darling.'

For four or five dazed, reeling, unbelieving seconds I sat motionless. Then I leapt to my feet,

swung round, knocked several glasses crashing to
the floor – the ritzy clientele of the Savoy were
certainly getting their money's worth tonight –
and faced Stella.

Stella! For a moment I could say nothing. I could
only stand and look – and look. She stood there,
dark and lovely and smiling, the old Stella of the
Malta days – only, there were tears in her eyes now.

Then I grabbed her. I hugged her till she cried
for mercy. Finally, I kissed her.

The gallery hadn't missed a thing. They were
right on the ball and this was their cue. We sat
down to a storm of hand-clapping.

'And they didn't get you after all?' I asked stupidly.

'Why should they have?' she smiled.

'Passière faked her message,' Nicky explained.
'There was no *MMR*, no armoured car. When he
jumped up, he must have knocked off the receiving switch. He'd hoped we would go after her and
then he'd contact his pals and they'd get the lot of
us. Only, it didn't quite work out that way. You
came back and his own pals – the guy in the
Heinkel – contacted him first.'

'Nicky picked me up that night,' Stella went on.
'He told me what had happened – about the sinking of the 149. I cried. Didn't I, Nicky? I cried all
night. I'm a fearful crybaby, really. Very second-
rate spy material.' She dabbed her eyes with a tiny
square of lace.

I smiled and turned to Nicky.

'So you looked Stella up after the war? Is that it?'

He grinned. 'Well, in a way.'

I looked at the rings on her left hand.

'So then,' I continued morosely, 'I suppose you got married?'

Stella smiled. 'Well, no, not exactly. You see, we always were – 1938, to be precise!'

My nervous system couldn't take much more. I'd just about used up all my reactions. I just sat there half-stunned, conscious that my face was turning a bright and glowing crimson.

'Sorry, Mac.' Nicky was apologetic. 'Couldn't even tell you. Had anyone known – our side, their side – our usefulness would have been at an end. We would have been a menace to our own people. I told you, Mac, often. You can't give hostages to fortune.'

Slowly, it all came back to me. I could see it all now and cursed myself for my blindness.

Their overdone casualness and offhandedness towards each other. The constant bickering, yet the unswerving loyalty and belief in each other – how familylike, I thought with chagrin. Nicky's strange behaviour when I suggested I might fall for her (I squirmed at that thought). His anger when I expressed distaste for her spying. The secret holding of hands. His increasingly haggard and worried appearance – God, I thought, how would I have felt if *my* wife had been in that position. Finally, his desperate eagerness to rescue her – strictly in defiance of all Special Service orders and, as far as he had known at the time, in the face of certain capture or death.

Without a word I pushed my chair away from the table and rose carefully to my feet. Slowly my leg came back and deliberately, and with great accuracy, I kicked myself.

The gallery, first-nighters to a man and obviously trained to a hair, applauded with great fervour. And as I sat down, I realized that the unbridled enthusiasm of the audience wasn't entirely on my behalf.

Laughter and tears and love walk always hand in hand. Stella and Nicky were kissing each other with a most unEnglish lack of restraint. They looked for all the world like a pair of newly-weds.

Which for me, of course, was exactly what they were.

The Jervis Bay

The second year of the war, as dark and sombre a year as Britain had ever known, was drawing steadily to its dark and sombre close. November, 1940, and behind lay the long agonizing months of hardship and suffering and crushing defeat, abandonment by our last allies in Europe, the wanton destruction of our cities and towns and thousands upon thousands of civilians, of the never-ending and always imminent threat of invasion by a ruthless and implacable enemy who would be content with nothing short of the annihilation of our country as an entity and a nation.

True, the crushing defeat was a thing of the past, albeit of the recent past: Hitler's all-conquering Panzer divisions had swept us out of Europe and only a miracle had spared the survivors who had found their way to the desolate beaches of Dunkirk. The collapse of France, also, was long an accomplished fact, and we had at least and at last the satisfaction of knowing precisely where we stood – alone.

But the Battle of Britain was still with us. Night after night, through the lengthening hours of darkness of October and November, the Luftwaffe's heavy bombers, seldom less than two hundred at a time, droned over our ports and cities and unloaded their cargoes indiscriminately over docks, factories and homes – but principally over homes. And the threat of invasion, the launching of the long-awaited operation 'Sealion' against our shores, was a looming peril that might at any hour of the night or day explode into devastating reality.

Britain, in that dark hour, was exactly in the position of a beleaguered garrison the remnants of whose army, all but destroyed in the field, have taken refuge behind the walls and barred the gates. But beleaguered garrisons can fall, and invariably do fall, if fear and despair destroy the will to survive or if constant attrition weakens the defenders to the point where continued defence and defiance becomes a physical impossibility, but most surely of all, they can be inexorably starved into surrender.

There was nothing to fear on the first score. Defiance burned like a flame, and with pikes, clubs and home-made petrol bombs the people of Britain were prepared to follow Churchill's injunction to fight for every beach and street and village in the country. But starvation and attrition was another matter altogether.

We had to have food or die. We had to have minerals and metals and chemicals for the manufacture of tanks and weapons for our weaponless armies, we had to have oil for the naval ships that guarded the shores, for the factories and the power stations, for the manufacture of petrol enough to keep in the air the handful of Hurricanes and Spitfires that alone stood between us and the savagery of the Luftwaffe.

The food, the oil and many of the most essential raw materials had to be imported into this beleaguered garrison; and there was only one way by which these could come – the sea. A garrison without any hope of relief, we were utterly dependent on the merchant ships that sailed upon this sea as our only remaining lifeline to the world that lay beyond. But lifelines can be cut. The Germans knew this as well as anyone.

They spared no effort to cut these lifelines, once and for all. Sabotage in foreign ports, bomber attacks above the sea, E-boats on the sea, U-boats under the sea – they threw in every weapon they possessed. But, at that time, their most deadly and devastating weapon of all was the raider – heavy cruisers and pocket battleships, big fast and powerful vessels that could be stopped by nothing less than a battleship of the line. An armed raider let loose among a convoy was prelude to a merciless and inevitable slaughter – the *Hipper*, for instance, had once fallen upon a defenceless convoy and sent eleven merchant ships to the bottom in less than an hour.

And now, with the collapse of France and the fall of Norway offering the enemy a thousand miles of Atlantic seaboard as operating base, and with the advent of winter storms and long winter nights affording almost unlimited opportunity to break out into the Atlantic, the menace had reached critical proportions. The raiders, with almost complete freedom of operation, sailed where they liked, struck where they chose and sank with impunity.

This impunity could have been removed, risks halved and effective counter-measures doubled if we had had bases nearer the scene of action: the country at large, no less than the Admiralty, was convinced of this. The use of certain ports in Southern Ireland, would have moved our outposts far west into the Atlantic, and the advantages gained, the scores of ships and thousands of lives saved, could have made all the difference between life and death. But Southern Ireland wasn't interested in the life or death of its neighbour (officially, that is – it would be most unfair to forget that thousands of its citizens volunteered for and served with distinction in our armed forces during the war) and categorically denied us the use of any port in Ireland. Far from offering us help in these, our darkest days, they were prepared to stand aside while the German raiders cut our lifeline to the outer world and brought us to defeat.

In Britain, in the latter half of 1940, the feeling against Ireland was intense: so it was particularly fitting that it should be an Irishman, Captain Edward Fogarty Fegen, who was to light the beacon of hope in the darkness, who was to show that we could live in spite of the lack of bases, that a convoy could survive even the savagery of a full-scale assault by a pocket battleship . . . Provided, of course, that there was always a Fegen to stand between the convoy and the enemy.

It was the evening of 5 November, 1940, and Convoy HX 84, in latitude 52° 45′ North, longitude 32° 13′ West – the very heart of the Atlantic – was steaming steadily, peacefully home to England. The sky was a cloudless blue: visibility was exceptional: light airs blew gently out of the south-east and the setting sun glittered across the burnished gold of a sea calm and quiet and smooth as the Atlantic almost never is.

In nine parallel lines, the big convoy slowly zig-zagged its way across the broad face of the Atlantic. Thirty-seven ships there were in all in this convoy – including eleven tankers – and the total value of its cargoes of food and machinery and oil quite beyond computation. Millions of pounds, many millions of pounds, but then the value was not to be reckoned in terms of money but in terms of the lives of those who sailed the cargoes home from Halifax, in the lives and the freedom of those who so eagerly awaited these desperately needed supplies.

Among these thirty-seven ships there were some which, for one reason or another, took the attention and the eye more often than the others. The New Zealand *Rangitiki*, for instance, 17,000 tons and the largest ship in the convoy: the *Puck*, at the other end of the scale, a tiny 1,000 ton vessel that had no business at all on those great waters: or the *Cornish City*, wearing the flag of the Convoy Commodore, Rear-Admiral Maltby. These caught the eye, and one or two others: but certainly no one paid much attention to two ships destined for a fame that has diminished but little with the passing of the years – the tanker *San Demetrio*, London and the Swedish motor vessel *Stureholm*, Gothenburg – or to the third, sailing steadily east and into immortality, the armed merchant cruiser *Jervis Bay*.

The *Jervis Bay*, the sole guardian and escort of all these ships, was in the middle of the convoy. Neither in appearance nor in fact was she calculated to inspire any confidence at all among the vessels she was supposed to protect. She was big – 14,000 tons – but in war size counts for little. What mattered was that she was old – built in 1922 – vulnerable, unarmoured, and equipped with only a handful of worn, weak and inaccurate 6-inch guns, twice as old as the *Jervis Bay* herself: as a man of war, as a fighting ship, she had nothing: but then again she had everything – she had Captain Fogarty Fegen.

Captain Fegen, a big, tough, 47 year-old bachelor Irishman, son of an admiral, grandson of a captain, already twice decorated for his gallantry, was in his usual position on the bridge when a ship was sighted far to the north, hull-down over the smooth, unbroken horizon. That ship had no business to be there, and at once the challenge started flickering out from the Aldis lamp on the bridge of the *Jervis Bay*.

The stranger made no reply, but kept steaming at high speed towards the convoy. A second challenge went out. That, too, went unanswered. Then a third – but after the third there was no need for more. Fegen had her now. The fox was in among the chickens.

It was the 10,000 ton, 30-knot pocket battleship *Admiral Scheer*, a powerful, heavily armoured raider equipped with six 11-inch guns of a phenomenal range, and a secondary armament of eight 5.9-inch guns. Only a *Nelson*, a *Rodney* or a *Hood* could have stopped her with certainty – nothing else. She was a killer against whom there was no defence and her helpless victims could only lie there waiting for her, waiting for the inevitable execution: her hull was heaving over the horizon now, and HX 84 could see the setting sun striking golden glints off the white waters piled high at her bow as she raced south under the maximum power of her great engines.

'Action Station' bells sounded aboard the *Jervis Bay* as the signal to the convoy fluttered up to her yardarm – 'Prepare to scatter'. Almost at the same moment, Rear-Admiral Maltby on the *Cornish City* gave the order for an emergency turn to starboard, away from the enemy: at once all the ships in the convoy heeled far over to port as they broke south-east under cover of a smoke screen.

All the ships – except one. The biggest smoke screen ever laid, Captain Fegen realized grimly, wasn't going to make the slightest difference to the *Admiral Scheer*. She would slice through that swirling curtain of smoke as if it didn't exist, pursue and cut the fleeing convoy to pieces. Smoke was not enough: the convoy had to have time, time to scatter and lose themselves in the great wastes of the Atlantic, time to wait for the protective blanket of night . . . Fegen pulled the *Jervis Bay* round to port under maximum rudder and headed straight for the *Admiral Scheer*.

Even before the *Jervis Bay* had straightened up on course, the *Admiral Scheer*, determined that it would not be baulked of its prey by this crazy gesture of defiance, opened up with its 11-inch guns. Some shells fell among the convoy. The *Rangitiki* was straddled but miraculously escaped: the tanker *San Demetrio*, then and later, was heavily hit, set on fire, abandoned, then later resighted, boarded and sailed home in triumph.

But the *Scheer*, at that moment, had no interest in the convoy, only in the big merchantman racing in on a collision course. Two ranging salvos fell one on either side of the armed merchant cruiser, dismaying testimony to the German reputation for gunnery of a quite phenomenal accuracy: the third salvo crashed solidly home into the hull.

In one stroke the foremast was shot away, the bridge all but destroyed, the director and rangefinder wrecked, the transmitting station, which controlled all the guns, knocked out of action and the guns themselves rendered useless for all but primitive hand control – the cables feeding in the electrical supplies had been completely severed.

The battle had not yet properly begun, but already the *Jervis Bay* was finished as a fighting unit. Kapitän Theodore Krancke of the *Admiral Scheer* knew that he had nothing more to fear from the big merchantman. He at once altered course to the east to overtake the fleeing convoy, only to find that his way was barred once more: the *Jervis Bay*, too, had put over her helm, and was again closing rapidly on a head-on collision course.

Savagely the *Admiral Scheer* lashed out at the crippled merchant cruiser that so infuriatingly baulked him of the retreating convoy. Not one shell or two, this time, but salvo after salvo, each shell 650 pounds of high-explosive steel, screamed across the calm ice-cold surface of the sea and smashed, pairs and threes at a time, into their target with devastating accuracy, killing, maiming and destroying, scything across the upper decks and superstructure in a murderous storm of bursting shrapnel or exploding deep inside the already mortally wounded *Jervis Bay*. There was no more thought, now, on the part of the Germans, of just silencing the *Jervis Bay*'s guns and bypassing her to the south: they meant to finish her off, swiftly and without mercy.

But the *Jervis Bay* was not to be so easily finished off. Impossibly, not only did she still survive, but she still held steadily on course, still making for the pocket battleship that was relentlessly hammering the life out of her. Great holes were now torn in her port side, above water level and below: the boiler room was severely damaged: the wireless room was gone: the bridge and superstructure had been hit again and again, and she was listing more and more heavily with the passing of each moment as rivers of water poured in through the gaping rents in her side.

Fogarty Fegen still stood on what shattered remnants were left of his wrecked and blazing bridge. In the first few minutes Fegen, like his ship, was wounded to death, but like his ship incredibly he survived and kept on closing with the enemy long after death should have claimed him.

He was terribly wounded. An exploding shell had blown his left arm off just below the shoulder, and the arterial blood was pumping out with every heartbeat: the agony must have been indescribable but Fegen ignored it. He still issued his orders calmly, concisely and with the courtesy that had always been his wont as he drove the *Jervis Bay* ever closer to the enemy, as he directed the firing of those ancient and pathetic guns whose useless shells fell into the sea miles short of the *Admiral Scheer.*

Another exploding shell, and the main steering controls were severed. At once Captain Fegen ordered the quartermaster back to the emergency steering position – whatever happened they must retain steering control, move in ever closer on the German battle cruiser. The bridge, burning more furiously than ever and beginning to buckle under the captain's feet, became completely untenable. Steadying himself with his one good arm, Fegen descended the twisted steel ladder and staggered aft, along the promenade deck, through the choking smoke and eddying flames, to the emergency bridge, every foot of his progress marked by a smeared trail of blood on the charred and blackened decks.

Arriving aft, Captain Fegen, his face now chalk-white and bloodless and wracked by that murderous pain to which he never once gave expression, found himself too weak to climb up to the control position: but he was still the captain, still in command, with no purpose left in life but to shorten the distance between himself and the *Admiral*

Scheer, to give the convoy every life-giving moment of grace he could so that they might make good their escape into the swiftly gathering dusk.

And thinking ever of the convoy, he ordered more smoke-floats to be dropped, to hide HX 84 from the *Scheer*. He ordered burning cordite charges to be thrown overboard, fresh crews to man the few guns still firing, in place of those men who lay dead around them. But even yet, those worn and useless guns could not reach the enemy.

Another 11-inch shell, another and another, and now the engine room was destroyed, the engines smashed and drowned under hundreds of tons of water. Fogarty Fegen no longer cared. A 14,000 ton ship travelling at maximum speed has tremendous way on her, and he knew that the *Jervis Bay* had more than enough way in reserve to keep her closing on the *Admiral Scheer* in the brief span of life that was left to both himself and his ship.

A deafening roar, a flash of searing flame and the after control position above Fegen's head vanished in the concussive blast of yet another detonating shell. Undaunted, this incredible man, blood still pouring from his shattered shoulder and head-wounds, lurched his dying way back through the smoke and the flames, intent on reaching the blazing bridge he had so lately abandoned, to continue the fight – if this ghastly massacre could be called a fight – from there.

But he never reached that shattered bridge again. Somewhere in the flames he was struck down by a bursting shell, and death must have been instantaneous for, by any medical standards, he was dead on his feet before that shell finally sheared the slender thread of life to which he had clung with such unbelievable courage and tenacity.

In the one brief hour of a November dusk, Fogarty Fegen won for himself the posthumous Victoria Cross and a name which will always be remembered, with that of Sir Phillip Sydney, as a symbol of defiance and an almost inhuman gallantry in the face of fearful odds. The Victoria Cross and an assured immortality – but probably Captain Fegen would have cared for neither. He had done his job. He had stolen from Kapitän Krancke of the *Admiral Scheer* those vital moments that were never to be regained, and thereby saved the greater part of the convoy.

Fegen was dead, but the victory was his. But not only Fegen's. Every man under his command had fought, till the guns had fallen silent and fighting was no longer possible, with the same gallantry as their captain. For most of them, the price of their magnificent defiance had been the same. Of the 260 of the crew, almost two hundred were already dead or terribly wounded and about to die.

Listing, sinking deeply by the stern and now all but stopped in the water, the *Jervis Bay*, still with shells crashing through the smoke and the flame that now consumed almost her entire length, was obviously about to go at any moment. Those who were left – and they were not many – abandoned the dying ship just minutes before she slid stern-first under the waves, taking with her all those in the sea too near or too weakened by wounds to resist the tremendous suction.

It is unlikely that any of the others who escaped would have survived for long – the *Admiral Scheer* made no attempt to pick them up – had not Captain Sven Olander, master of the Swedish vessel *Stureholm*, conscious of the great debt they owed to the survivors of the ship that had saved the convoy, ignored all orders and turned back in the darkness of the night to search for the men of the *Jervis Bay*. It was an act of the utmost courage, for all night long the *Admiral Scheer*, robbed of her prey, was prowling around the area, firing off star shells as she hunted for the now far scattered members of HX 84. But the great risk Olander took was justified over and over again: they found and rescued from the freezing night waters of the Atlantic no fewer than sixty-five survivors.

A hopeless sacrifice, many people later called the loss of the *Jervis Bay*. Sheer senseless destruction to send in a cockleshell like *the Jervis Bay* against the might of a pocket battleship, a folly and a bravado that amounted to nothing less than madness. No doubt such people are right. No doubt it was madness, but one feels that Fegen and his men would have been proud to be numbered among the madmen of this world.

And one feels, too, that it would be unwise, to say the least, to express such harsh sentiments in the hearing of any of the members of the crews of the ships of Convoy HX 84 that came safely home again because Fogarty Fegen and the men of the *Jervis Bay* had moved out into the path of the *Admiral Scheer* and died so that they might live.

The Black Storm

I don't know how much old Glass was worth. Come to that, I don't suppose he knew himself. But he was as rich as Croesus, that's a fact.

But Croesus or no, peer of the realm or no, he was still the same old Duncan Glass and hardly a week went by but he came down from the Big House to my harbour office to pass the time of day with me. But he'd something on his mind that Saturday – a sunny breezy morning in late June.

He got his pipe drawing well, then looked round the harbour, at the waves sparkling in the sunshine, at the mast-tops of the fishing boats dancing in the breeze. Then he turned to me, direct as always.

'Tom,' he said quietly, 'what do you think of them? Really think of them, I mean.'

'Think of who?'

'You know damn well who! The Tallons, of course.' He jerked his pipe stem in the direction of the two men working round an old varnished yellow pine fishing boat. 'Look at them. A holiday, every other man going to the Games, and there they are, still at it.'

'They seem to like working,' I said, mildly enough.

Lord Glass glared at me. 'I didn't ask you . . .'

'All right, all right,' I said quickly. 'Well, if you must know, I like old John Tallon and his son.'

Glass glared at me again. 'No one else does.'

'No?' I nodded through the window, then caught Glass's arm as he reached for the door handle. 'Leave her be, Duncan. What harm can she come to?'

'Aye, maybe you're right,' he muttered. 'For the moment anyway.'

He stood in silence and watched the young girl walking down the quay, dark hair and red kilt blowing in the breeze, one hand holding canvas, paints, and brushes while she waved to the Tallons with the other. As she came opposite the Tallons' boat, the *Jeannie*, a young man jumped up on the quay, smiled and spoke to her. Moments later he was sitting on a bollard, looking at the canvas the young girl was showing him. The black and flaxen heads were very close together.

'I don't like it.' I could hear Glass's teeth biting hard on his pipe stem, and his voice was kind of savage and quiet at the same time. 'I don't like it at all.'

'What you mean is you don't like them.' I knew how old Duncan Glass felt about Mairi – since her parents had been killed his 11-year-old granddaughter was the only person he had left in the world – but I felt he was being a bit hard. 'Why don't you be honest about it, Duncan?'

'Can you blame me?' he said angrily.

'No more than I blame any of the others. You're just as bad as they are. Forty-five years in the city of London, and you're still a West Coaster at heart. The Tallons are East Coasters. Oil and water never did mix.'

Glass growled deep in his throat, but I held up my hand.

'And you're just as nosy as the others. The Tallons are mysterious, and you don't like mystery. But if they care to sail through the Caledonian Canal and change the *Jeannie*'s registration marks in Skye so that they don't know where they come from, surely that's their business. It's certainly none of ours.'

'You talk like an East Coaster yourself,' Glass said sourly. 'Admit it man, they're a close, stand-offish couple.'

I admitted nothing. I knew he was wrong, but I knew I couldn't convince him. I knew, too, what really rankled with Lord Glass and the others . . .

The Tallons were far and away the best fishermen in Inverglas. Only six months in the village and already they caught more every day than any two other boats out together, more than men who had fished these sounds and banks all their lives. It was natural, I suppose, that the men should resent that, the seven other skippers who sailed Lord Glass's boats on a profit-sharing basis. It was natural that they should stand around on the quay, sullen and morose, after a poor day's haul, while the spotted olive green and white of cod, the silver blue of mackerel spilled from the *Jeannie*'s overflowing baskets as they were hoisted up for weighing.

However, I couldn't very well say this to Glass, and I knew he thought I'd nothing more to say in their defence. He changed the conversation, slightly.

'Mairi's down here pretty often, isn't she?'

'As often as the boats are in. Otherwise she's usually over by Sunda Bay. Always painting. A very gifted young lassie you've got there, Duncan.'

'She's all that.' Lord Glass permitted himself a proud smile, then remembered what he was about. 'She sees young Tallon quite often, eh?'

'Now and again.' I was feeling uncomfortable. 'When he's not working.'

'No idea what they talk about?'

'As a matter of fact, I have.' I was on better ground here. 'Always about painting. Heard the two of them at it the other day. Young Tallon was telling her how important it was that she should always *see* – see lines and depths and shadow and above all colour. He was pointing out a particular part of the village or harbour or sea or sky and asking her to describe it for him – just to find out how much she saw, and how much she didn't. I'm sure he helps her.'

'What the devil does he know about painting?' Glass snorted. 'Ignorant young lout who's never . . .'

'How the devil do you know . . .' I started angrily, but Glass recognized the signs from 60 long years ago.

'Sorry, Tom, sorry: let's not fight about it. But I still don't like it. It's gone far enough. I'm going to stop it.'

'Mairi's safer here than in Sunda Bay. If the tide . . .'

'MacArthur' – that was his chauffeur – 'is always with her. She'll come to no harm. See you next week, Tom.'

After he'd gone – and taken Mairi with him – I got to thinking about the Tallons. They were a queer pair all right, father and son. Always they were together, John Tallon with his broad shoulders and grey beard and the useless leg swinging between the crutches, and his son, Michael, half a head again taller than his father, with long blond straight hair and a queer faraway look in the washed-out blue of his eyes.

* * *

Always they were together – always. It didn't matter whether they were out fishing, or mending lines, or getting bait or just digging in the kitchen garden behind the little cottage they had rented on the hill, they were as inseparable as Siamese twins. They worked like Trojans, almost inhumanly hard, kept themselves strictly to themselves – and were the most disliked folk in town. Until, that is, the night of the Black Storm.

The Black Storm. It came in the early evening of the day of the Glasgow Fair, in July, and Inverglas was a ghost town for the night. It was the big day of the year in Dalbreath, seven or eight miles away across the bay – gala fete, sideshows, and a dance that lasted far into the morning. Every person who could be there was there.

But not everybody had gone – not quite. I stayed in my harbour office, because the weather forecast had been a bad and bitter one – Force 9 winds with gale seas and thunder – and I had to be there, all the time, in case some ship in distress might be looking for help or shelter.

And the Tallons were there, too – it didn't need any clairvoyant to know that *they* wouldn't be in Dalbreath. It wasn't just that they knew that they weren't wanted there: the Tallons never spent any money on amusement, and not a ha'penny more on drink – and everybody knew you couldn't enjoy a good old-time dance without a dram or two in the right place. Come to think of it, I don't suppose that helped their popularity any – West Highland fishermen tend to look a bit askance at a man too mean to put his hand in his pocket for a drink.

The Tallons had just finished pumping out the *Jeannie* when the rain started. It didn't just rain – the black skies opened and it came down in pailfuls.

At once the two men turned up their collars and hurried up the quay as fast as old John could hobble, but that wasn't very fast. I slid open the door of the office as they stumbled by and shouted on them to come in.

They were glad enough to come, I can tell you. As I closed the door behind them, old John sunk into a chair and let his breath go in a long gasp.

'Thank you, Mr Burnett, thank you.' He looked out at the sky, already dark almost as a tomb, and shook his head. 'It's going to be a wild night.'

'It's going to be all that.' I nodded at the stove. 'Just brewed a pot of tea. Plenty for three.'

John Tallon hesitated, then smiled. 'It's very kind of you, Mr Burnett.'

But we never had that cup of tea. I was just about to pour it when the door crashed open and there was Lord Glass himself, his face wild, grey with exhaustion and his breath coming in great heaving gasps.

'Where are all the men, Tom, the fishermen?' It took him three long breaths to jerk this out. 'I can't see . . .'

'They're all over at Dalbreath, Duncan. You know that. Fair Friday. What in the name of God . . .' I broke off suddenly, because I already knew. 'Mairi?'

'Aye.' He nodded heavily, his face sunk in his hands.

'Sunda Bay?'

He nodded again, said nothing.

'And the tide making more than half already!' I could feel the cold horror in my blood. 'But MacArthur, the man who looked after her . . .'

'Gone to Dalbreath, and never a word to me,' The spirit was back for a moment, the voice savage. 'When I see him again . . .' He left the sentence unfinished.

'You're sure she's there?'

'I know. When the storm came on, I looked for her. Couldn't find her. Drove to Sunda, saw her pony there.' His fists were clenched, his chest still heaving. 'I ran down the cliff path – but it was too late. The beach is cut off already and the water wild.'

'You saw her?'

'I saw her. Shouted to her to get as far up the cliff as she could. Then I ran all the way here.'

The wind was booming outside now, rising up to gale force. How long, I thought frantically, could a little girl hang on in that. Men, ropes, but no, that overhang of the Sunda cliff . . .

I started and turned as a sudden blast of wind blew papers all over the office floor. Michael

Tallon had the door open, his father just behind him, crutches already under his arms. It was John Tallon who spoke.

'We'll be back in the half-hour,' he said quietly. 'You can come if you like – but it's a wild night.'

And, my heaven, it *was* a wild night. The *Jeannie* rolled and pitched her way across the bar as if every shuddering plunge into the troughs was going to be her last, but she was a tough old craft with a Gleniffer diesel and John knew how every single combing wave was setting towards us even although it was as black as the Earl of Hell's waist-coat. He handled that boat as if he had been born with a tiller under his arm.

We had to quarter our way round Sunda Point – if we had gone broadside into any of these steep-walled troughs we'd have broached to and foundered in a matter of moments – and, by Jove, it's a trip I don't want ever to do again. What with the howling of the wind, the thunder beginning to rumble, the rain and the spray tearing at our faces and the wild staggering of the *Jeannie* – well, as I say, once in a lifetime was once too many.

But we made it, and in a few minutes we were running into Sunda Bay, into the comparative quiet of the water behind the point.

We were maybe 40 yards off the cliff – the sand was already deep under water – when John shoved the Gleniffer into reverse and shouted on

Michael to let go the anchor. Surefooted as a cat in the darkness, picking his way with uncanny precision through the boxes, lines and ropes that lay always in the same tidy positions on deck, Michael Tallon moved to the bows and 30 seconds later the *Jeannie* was anchored head-on to the mouth of the bay, the Gleniffer just ticking over to take part of the strain, the counter swinging wildly only two or three feet from the face of the cliff.

It wasn't really a cliff at the bottom – but it wasn't far off it. Halfway up the rock bulged out a wicked overhang, and it was just below this that we saw Mairi right away, her white blouse plain against the darkness of the rock. She was hanging on to a spur for dear life, and in the sudden lulls between the gusts of wind we could hear the wee soul crying.

We all waited for Michael to fetch her – it wasn't a difficult jump ashore, nor the climb too dangerous for an active young man like himself. Old John couldn't go – not with only one leg. I suppose Glass or myself could have gone, but don't forget neither of us would ever see 65 again.

I don't think I was ever more dumbfounded in my life than when I saw Michael hesitating, making no move at all to go – and I'll never forget the anguished expression on his father's face – I was by his shoulder – as he sat there, just watching him.

'You despicable young coward!' Duncan Glass, now that he saw his granddaughter still safe, was back on balance again and his voice was the lash of a whip. 'You're a damned good man – when you're sitting with a child's sketchbook in your hand. But if I ever see you again within a mile . . .'

He choked in anger, made to push past Michael, then sat down with a gasp on a coil of rope as an iron arm caught him by the lapels and forced him off his feet. Michael Tallon paused only to say a few soft words to his father, bent his ear to the reply, then leapt ashore.

Not quite three feet, yet he almost missed it. His ankle seem to give under him, he tottered back wildly on his heels, his arms flailing, then recovered his balance at the last moment, caught hold of a projecting rock and started climbing.

I didn't see all of the climb – it was too dark for that – but what I did see I wouldn't have believed. I don't *think* I've ever seen a man so clumsy on a rock face. Cat-footed as a tightrope walker on a rolling deck, he was quite lost on a cliff-face. He fumbled and pawed and slipped his way up to where the little girl lay crying, and my heart was never out of my mouth. But reach her he did, caught her in one arm – the poor wee girl was near exhaustion by this time – and made his way slowly, awkwardly, down again. He was so engrossed in what he was doing that I'll swear he'd have stepped into the sea if old John hadn't shouted a warning.

The rain had almost stopped now, and the wind changed – changed so that the stern of the *Jeannie* had moved out seven or eight feet. Duncan it was

who caught up a heaving line and threw an end
to Michael so that he could pull the stern close in.
The line hit Michael on the chest, and fell into the
water before he could clutch it.

Duncan Glass pulled in the line, coiled it and
flung it once more. Michael lifted his hand to
catch it as it whistled towards him, but again he
missed it – it seemed to strike the back of his wrist
and glanced off into the sea.

'For God's sake man, are you blind?' Glass
shouted in exasperation. He hauled in the rope,
but I took it from him, and threw it carefully so
that it fell over Michael's shoulders. My mouth
was dry, I felt as cold as the tomb.

'He *is* blind, Duncan,' I said, and my voice was
only a trembling whisper. 'He's completely stone
blind.'

And he was. The rest we learned later that
night, sitting before a great fire in Glass's library,
stiff tots of whisky in our hands.

'We were both in the same train smash, Lord
Glass,' old John was saying. He seemed to be glad
to be talking, glad that the secrecy and conceal-
ment were all over. 'That's how I got my leg –
well, shortened a bit. And Michael – he got hurt at
the same time. He – well, you've seen, he doesn't
see too well.'

Doesn't see too well, I thought – the boy moved
in a world of utter dark! The longer I sat there,

the clearer things became – and the more I writhed in shame, for myself and my people. No wonder the boy had never left his father's side. No wonder everything on the deck of the *Jeannie* had always been in exactly the same place. No wonder, now, that he moved so surefootedly aboard in the dark – day and night were all the same to Michael Tallon. And no wonder that he had had little Mairi describe everything so minutely to him – not only had he wanted to 'see' the new world he was living in, but he himself, we found, was an artist, just finishing his final year in the School of Art and she had represented for him the one place where his real interest in life lay – or had lain.

'But good God, man,' – it was Glass speaking – 'Why did you never tell us?'

'Because there is – or was – hope for him yet.' Old John sounded suddenly tired. 'They told us in Glasgow that there's a man in Baltimore, in Johns Hopkins Hospital, who's a genius in the particular eye surgery Michael needs. So – well, we were trying to save a little money to go there and pay for the operation.'

The simplicity of it all, the magnificence of it all, left Glass and myself with nothing to say. A one-legged man, a blind boy, the bitter toil from the dawn till long beyond the sunset – no, this lay beyond tears . . . After a while, Glass said weakly: 'But you could still have told us.'

'And lost my fishing licence? A blind crew? Where would the money have come from then?'

'I don't know, I don't know at all.' Glass drained his whisky tumbler, sat still for a moment, then smiled, a long slow smile. 'But, by God, I know where it's coming from now.'

Michael hasn't had his operation yet – but the last letter from John said that the preliminary tests were almost over. And when it does come – well, I know he'll carry with him the hopes and prayers of every soul in Inverglas.

The Good Samaritan

It wanted almost an hour to sunset when I took the hill road out of Tarnford, but already the brief spring twilight was all but gone. The sky above was dark not with the coming of night but with deep-piled banks of thundercloud that stretched its purple-black shroud over hills and valleys to the limits of the horizon. The rain, thick gleaming metallic rods in my headlights, battered against the windscreen, bounced inches high off the smoking roadway ahead, and churned into a miniature boiling cauldron, the water trapped in the upturned hub-cap of the spare wheel on the engine bonnet.

I didn't really care about the weather, about the rain, about the dazzling electric blue of the lightning that left the outline of its jagged path imprinted on the retina of the eyeball long seconds after the flash had gone or the continuous artillery rumble of the thunder overhead. I didn't care, because I was too tired to care. I'd been up all the previous night trying to save one of the Colonel's thoroughbred mares, and had just reached home when a panic call from Tarnford, where the big cattle fair had been held that day, had had me on my way again. Foot-and-mouth, they had suspected. A false alarm, but I hadn't taken any chances. Eleven solid hours in the pens, and now I was exhausted.

Perhaps it was because of the exhaustion, perhaps because of the rain streaming down the windscreen, that I didn't see the swinging red lanterns on the road before me until it was almost too late. I stamped on the brake; brought the Land Rover to a sliding halt, and stuck my head through the side-screen.

'What the devil are you fools trying to do?' I said angrily. 'Get yourselves killed or what?' I peered at the approaching figure, caught a gleam of wet cape in the reflected light from my headlamps. 'Police, is it?'

'Yes, sir.' The voice was curt, impersonal. 'May we see your driving licence, please?'

'My driving licence?' I suppose my voice sounded a bit testy, but as a vet I'd been too long accustomed to share with doctors and ministers of religion a comparative immunity from the attentions of the police. 'Why on earth – ' I broke off, as memory came flooding back. 'Of course! Sellers and Riordan.'

Sellers and Riordan. They'd talked about nothing else in the market all day, even the foot-

and-mouth had come a very poor second as a topic of interest. With reason. In six short days Sellers and Riordan had become the most talked-about pair in England. In seven brief days they had established themselves the reputation of the two most ruthless, most murderous criminals at large in Britain. In seven brief days they had held up a bank in Stepney, killed the manager, wounded a cashier, shot down a policeman who had tried to stop their escape, been arrested after a desperate struggle, remained in custody exactly 24 hours, then escaped, leaving behind them a dead warder, and another who might live or die.

And now they were supposed to be in the neighbourhood. They had been traced through Amesbury and Frome, had been seen in Glastonbury and now all Devon north of the Moor and Somerset west of the Quantocks were alive with police and an estimated 1200 troops, every man armed. But on Exmoor, in this weather, 12,000 wouldn't have been too many.

'Yes, sir, Sellers and Riordan.' The policeman's voice, more friendly now, brought me back to the present. 'Your licence, please.'

I handed it over and he nodded.

'Mr Cartwright. Thought I recognized you, sir. Going far?'

'Home. Lipscombe.'

'Lipscombe, eh? It's a fair way.' He looked at me, but I couldn't see the expression on his face. 'You'll watch your step, sir?'

'They're as near as that, you think?' Instinctively, I peered into the surrounding darkness, trying to pierce the slanting curtains of rain.

'Near enough,' he said grimly. 'A constable saw them outside Tiverton, just over an hour ago.'

'He could have been mistaken.' I was trying to reassure myself, I knew. 'Five hundred others are supposed to have seen them today also.'

'The other 500 didn't get a bullet in the shoulder,' he said unemotionally. 'So be careful, Mr Cartwright. No stopping. No lifts – not even to your own grandmother.'

'The level crossings?' I tried to keep the anxiety out of my voice. 'Three of them between here and Lipscombe. If the gates are shut . . .'

'No.' The policeman shook his head positively. 'Too obvious. Riordan's far too cagey to try to board a stopped car there.'

'But if he does . . . ?'

'Then it's curtains for Riordan. There's a platoon of soldiers with machine-pistols at every crossing in North Devon. You won't see them. But they'll be there all right.'

No doubt the policeman was right. No doubt there were hidden guards at the first crossing I came to, but as I sat there in the darkness and lessening rain, engine turned off so that I could listen the more intently while I waited for the goods train to come through, the knowledge didn't make me feel any the more happy. I kept turning and twisting constantly in my seat, pulling my muffler high around my neck. I could not forget how the warder had died: he had been garrotted. It would have been just as easy for them to knock him out, but they had garrotted him. That would have been Riordan's work. A wild animal, many called him, an animal devoid of all pity and humanity and fear.

The train took an eternity to pass, but pass it eventually did, and I was on my way even as the gates opened, accelerating to maximum revs through all the lower gears. I kept to the middle of the road, occasionally swerving to right or left as some imaginary figure or shadow appeared to resolve itself vaguely in the rain still lancing diagonally down through the glare of my headlights. I was rattled. I was more than rattled. I was scared, badly scared.

The second level crossing was open and then I was on the twisting, hilly five-mile stretch that lay between there and Hurford, the station that served Lipscombe.

The road was absolutely deserted. I hadn't seen a cyclist, a car, or pedestrian since I'd left Tarnford. The reason wasn't far to seek. The western regional radio programme had been interrupted by constant warnings throughout the day, and no one was abroad that night. Fear lay heavy over the land. Even the houses looked afraid, the front doors shut – and doubtless barred – with the windows heavily curtained.

It was near the top of that long rise before you dip down to Hurford that I saw him – first an indistinct barely moving blur by the roadside, a blur that, as I approached, resolved itself into the figure of a man crawling slowly, painfully along the side of the road. Crawling, I realized in horror. He was coming downhill towards me, his head hanging low and shaking stupidly from side to side. Even as I approached, my hands ivory-knuckled on the wheel and staring at him in a kind of sick fascination, he flopped over on to the grass verge and lay quite still, one arm outflung on the road, his face up to the night sky.

Anger overcame fear. I could not doubt that Riordan and Sellers had passed this way, and left their mark. I braked violently, jumped out of the Land Rover while it was still moving and bent over the still pathetic figure.

'The good Samaritan,' a jeering voice said behind me. 'Just stand up, sucker, and keep quite still.'

I stood up and I kept quite still. A tall thin man had appeared from nowhere, and he was standing now in the light of my headlamps, a pistol in his hand: I was enough of a movie addict to know that the clumsy cylinder attached to the muzzle of the pistol was a silencer. I was aware that the man

I had seen crawling along had jumped briskly to his feet behind me.

'Riordan and Sellers,' I said unemotionally. There was no fear in me at the moment: but I knew it would come later.

'None other, sucker,' the tall man agreed. 'I'm Riordan, he's Sellers. Into the car and start driving. You've a couple of back-seat passengers.'

'There's no back seat. It's a Land Rover.'

'All the better. Get in.'

Even if I hadn't known who he was, there was something in that voice that made for unquestioning obedience. I got in, while Riordan clambered over the two seats to my left and Sellers scrambled over the tailgate and through the back screens. Both had guns, and one gun was on me all the time.

'On your way. But take it easy. I want to talk to you.'

Carefully, without any fumbling but like a man in a dream, I started the Land Rover. Riordan's voice reached me above the sound of the engine as we moved off.

'Name, mister?'

'Cartwright.'

'You seem a pretty cool customer, Cartwright. Not thinking of doing anything clever, are you?'

'No.'

'What's your job?'

'Vet – veterinary surgeon.'

'Where do you live?'

'Lipscombe.'

'About four miles from here?'

'About that . . . What are you going to do with me?'

'Shut up.' His voice was expressionless. 'How far is Tarnmouth beyond that?' Tarnmouth was a tiny fishing village.

'About the same again. Four miles.'

'That's where we're going. All of us.'

I said nothing. I was trying to think desperately of what I might do, but the fear was beginning to well back and thought, constructive thought, wouldn't come. All I could think was that I had two ruthless murderers behind me, murderers with guns and an utter disregard for human life.

'Why are you going to Tarnmouth?' I asked. My voice was no longer steady.

'To catch a boat, Mr Cartwright.'

And then I remembered. Riordan was an Irishman, a Kerryman. He had friends, the police knew that, but they didn't know he had friends of that kind – willing to take the risk of rendezvousing with him and slipping him across the St George's Channel at night. And once in the hilly wilds of Cork and Kerry . . . That was as far as that line of thought got when another, and dreadful one, supplanted it. They could never let me live and give this information to the authorities. As sure as the sun would rise next morning, they were going to kill me.

Riordan was speaking again.

'How long have you lived here, Cartwright?'

'Seven years.'

'And a vet, eh? Everyone knows you?'

'I suppose so.'

'Fine. You're our safe conduct, Cartwright. Nobody will ever suspect the good healer. But remember this, and remember it good. If we're stopped, you're not to mention any place or person whatsoever by name. Understand?'

'I'm afraid I . . .'

'Look, Cartwright. If the police stop you and you volunteer the information that you're going to Timbuctoo Farm or been to see Mr Smith the Grocer and there's no Timbuctoo Farm or Smith the Grocer, they're going to get very suspicious, aren't they? So as little as possible – and nothing I can't check on.'

He was shrewd, all right, Riordan. The thought had never even occurred to me.

'What are all these sacks for, Cartwright?' Riordan was speaking again. 'Vets usually carry these?'

'Quite often. For sick animals and . . .'

'All right,' he interrupted. 'They'll cover us fine. You're carrying sick animals, if anyone asks. Remember, if we're stopped, I can see every flicker of expression on your face in the driving mirror. And the point of the gun is three inches from your back.'

The third set of level-crossing gates were closed, to let through the evening train. As I braked, John Howarth, the station master, came hurrying up.

'I thought it was you, Peter. Mary's coming off this train. Will you take her home? It's a filthy night, and with these two damned murderers around I . . .'

'Of course, I will,' I said. 'Tell her to wait in the bus shelter on the other side.'

'Thank you, boy.' He looked closely at me. 'You're looking a bit under the weather, you know. Too much – sorry, here she comes.' He hurried off, and we could hear the train approaching in the distance.

'Mary, eh?' Riordan murmured from under the sacks. 'Friend of yours, hey?'

'Yes,' I said shortly. 'And I'm not going to pick her up.'

'You are, you know.'

'Do you think I'm going to let you two damned murderers . . .'

'You said you would. If you don't, after promising, they're going to be as suspicious as hell when she tells the station master.'

'I don't give a damn. You can't make me do it.'

'Of course, she doesn't have to tell the station master – by the way, is he a friend of hers too?'

'Her father.'

'So. Well, Mr Cartwright, where's this bus shelter?'

'A hundred yards or so beyond the line.'

'And buses this time of night?'

Like a fool I answered: 'No'.

'So the shelter's deserted,' Riordan said softly. 'I've got a silencer and she could lie there for hours. No suspicions.'

Three minutes later I pulled up by the shelter. Mary came running out, pulled open the door of the Land Rover and jumped inside, tendrils of dark wet hair clinging to her neck and cheek, but cheerful and smiling as always.

'Hullo, Peter! Am I glad to see you tonight! The thought of walking home . . .' She broke off and peered at me. 'Why, whatever in the world is the matter, Peter?'

'Move over to the middle seat, Mary.' Fear for her had driven all fear for myself, and my mind was working at last. I thought I saw a glimmer of hope, no more than a desperate chance: but then I was a desperate man.

She moved slowly across, staring at me.

'I'm afraid I have a bad shock for you, darling,' I said. I put my arms round her slender shoulders, felt them stiffening under my pressure, sensed rather then saw the widening of the eyes. 'You've heard of Riordan and Sellers?'

She nodded dumbly.

'They're right behind us, darling – and they have guns in their hand.'

She said nothing, just turned slowly in her seat then put her hand to her mouth to stifle a frightened shuddering sigh as she saw the gun, the pale gleam of a face in the gloom.

'No screaming, young lady,' Riordan said quickly and quietly. 'This is a gun. Drive on Cartwright – and don't blame your friend, lady. If he hadn't stopped . . .' He explained briefly, then went on thoughtfully: 'Darling this, darling that, darling the next thing. She really does appear to be your friend, Cartwright.'

'Damn you to hell, Riordan,' I said savagely. 'She's my fiancée and now you've . . .'

'Your fiancée, eh? Well, well, well.' His voice changed. 'How do I know she's your fiancée?'

'What the devil does it matter . . . ?'

'It matters a lot. I never trust anybody or anything. Engaged? Ring?'

'Yes.'

'What's it like?'

'Emerald, four diamonds.'

Riordan stretched his hand. 'Show me.'

Wordlessly, Mary struggled to get it off her finger. God, I thought, she was behaving magnificently. She passed the ring back to Riordan, who struck a match, glanced at it and handed it back.

'Well, well,' he said softly. 'Love's young dream. The perfect set-up, eh, Sellers. Who's going to question love's young dream?'

There was a police block at the entrance to Lipscombe. Again there were red swinging lamps with, in the background, a truck across the street as a roadblock. On either side of the road I could see two policemen, strangers to me, mounted on their red-painted 100mph Thunderbird Twin Triumphs. They had that indefinable look of all motor cycle policemen – medium height, lean, very tough, very competent. But it was Sergeant Wynne who approached me. With the possible exception of Ainsworth, the young Vicar, Wynne was my best friend in Lipscombe.

'Evening, Pete,' he smiled. His torch reached across my seat, lit up Mary's face. 'Oh, hullo.'

'Evening, George,' I interrupted. 'What's all the cloak-and-dagger stuff for?' I nodded at the policemen on their motor cycles, the truck across the road, felt the hairs on the back of my neck stand on end as I felt the pressure of Riordan's silencer against the base of my spine. 'Looking for our wandering boys, Riordan and Sellers?'

'We are indeed,' Wynne said grimly. 'Suppose you've seen nothing, Pete.'

'Sorry,' I shrugged. 'All quiet between here and Tarnmouth. I don't envy you your job on a night like this.'

'Me neither,' Wynne said feelingly. 'Wish I was up looking for a double-twenty in the "Horse and

Plough".' We were both members of the local darts team. 'See you up there tonight, perhaps, Pete?'

'Perhaps, perhaps not.' I shrugged and grinned, knowing that Riordan was watching every slightest change of my expression in the driving mirror. 'There's a dance on in Tarnmouth. May be the small hours before we . . .' I broke off, put my arm round Mary's shoulders and squeezed: she nestled her dark head against my shoulder. 'Well, you know how it is, George.'

'Yes.' He took out his handkerchief, wiped some rain off his face and grinned back at me. 'Married myself, but I know how it is. Be seeing you, Pete.'

'Be seeing you.' I waited till the truck had backed out of the way, let in the clutch and moved off. Riordan stirred in the darkness.

'Not bad, Cartwright, not bad at all.' His tone changed, became soft and menacing. 'Why did you mention Tarnmouth, damn you?'

'Don't be such a bloody fool,' I said wearily. 'The only road out of Lipscombe leads there.'

We drove there in complete silence. I drove there in low gear most of the way, only once changing into top. It made for rather a noisy journey, but the low gear suited the road, the noise suited me. Every yard of the four miles I feared Riordan would order me to stop the Land Rover and take over himself: and then for Mary and myself there would only be the long sleep in the nearest ditch or behind the nearest convenient hedgerow. But the order to stop came only when we moved on to the Tarnmouth jetty.

'Far enough,' Riordan said harshly. He was almost there now, and the strain was beginning to tell, even on him. 'Kill the motor.'

I put my foot on the clutch, slipped the gear lever silently into first, switched off the ignition key, placed my right hand across the telltale red ignition light, switched the ignition on again and waited. The handbrake was off.

'Don't move, either of you,' Riordan warned. He was quite safe: the edge of the jetty was only 15ft away and deep water beyond. We couldn't escape that way.

I stared in the rear mirror, saw the pale gleam of light as they lifted the screens above the tail-gate, heard the metallic scuffle of a boot against the tailgate, and pressed the self-starter at the same instant.

Everything happened in a moment of time. The Land Rover jerked forward violently for a couple of feet before the engine stalled, Riordan and Sellers, swearing viciously, fell heavily to the ground behind, and the darkness and silence of the night was abruptly broken as two powerful headlights behind blazed into life at the same instant as clutches were let in and the twin cylinder engines of the powerful motor bikes caught with a throaty roar.

Riordan and Sellers had no chance. They were still struggling to their feet, blinded by the lights, when the motor bikes hit them: and before they could get up again four powerful policemen, piling out of the car immediately behind, had fallen on them with batons swinging.

'Beautifully, done, Pete, beautifully done indeed.' It was Sergeant Wynne talking, affecting not to notice the almost uncontrollable trembling of my arms and legs. 'We'll have that game of darts tonight yet – after a few pints. Tell me all.'

I told him, and at the end he turned to smile down coldly at a dazed and handcuffed Riordan.

'Mr Cartwright here had a unique opportunity of studying that young lady's engagement ring. He must have watched another ring being slipped on beside it, for practice like, at least 20 times before her wedding: and Mr Cartwright was the best man. It was hardly likely,' Wynne finished drily, 'that the Vicar's wife was going to go out all night dancing with another man only 48 hours after her wedding.'

Postscript

Rewards and Responsibilities of Success

Some time in 1954 the *Glasgow Herald* ran a short story competition. I had no writing aspirations – I won't say literary aspirations, for there are a considerable number of people who stoutly maintain that I never had and still don't have any literary aspirations – and no hope.

However the hundred pounds first prize was a very considerable lure for a person who had no money at all. I went ahead and entered anyway, with a West Highland sea story carrying the title *The 'Dileas'*. I won and was approached by Ian Chapman, the present chairman of Collins, the publishers, who asked me if I would write a novel. To everybody's surprise, Collins remain my publishers still. After twenty-seven years.

During those twenty-seven years I have written twenty-seven books, fourteen screenplays, and numerous magazine and newspaper articles. It has been, and remains, a fair enough way of earning a living. I have been called a success, but 'success', in its most common usage, is a relative term which has to be applied with great caution, especially in writing.

Quantification is far from being all. Some of the most 'successful' books, magazines, and newspapers in publishing history have beggared description when one tries to describe the depths to which they have descended. Enlightenment may not be my forte but, then, neither is depravity.

It is difficult to say what effect one's books have had, what degree of success or failure they have achieved. Consider, for instance, the reactions of those who had the debatable privilege of being on the *Glasgow Herald*'s editorial board at the time when those short stories of long ago were under consideration.

Some may feel, or have felt, a mild degree of satisfaction that they had the foresight or acumen to pick on someone who was not to prove a total dud: all too many writers produce one story and then are heard of no more. Others on the board may have felt a profound indifference. Still others, gnashing their figurative teeth, may have rued the day they launched on his way, a writer whose style, they felt or feel, in no way matched the high standard set itself by Scotland's premier newspaper. I shall never know.

The effect on the reading public is equally hard to gauge. I did write a couple of books which I thought might be judged as being meaningful or significant but from readers' reactions I was left in no doubt that the only person who shared this opinion was myself. I should have listened to Sam Goldwyn's dictum that messages are for Western Union.

I have since then concentrated on what I regarded as pure entertainment although I have discovered a considerable gulf may lie between what I regard as entertainment and others' ideas on the subject.

I receive a fairly large mail and most of it is more than kindly in tone. I am aware that this does not necessarily reflect an overall consensus of approval: I am essentially a non-controversial writer and people who habitually sign themselves 'Indignant' or 'Disgusted' of Walthamstow or wherever, don't read my books in the first place, or if they do, don't find the contents worthy of disparaging comment.

The effects of writing on myself, of course, I know fairly well although I'm aware that, even here, there may be room for blind misappraisal. The main benefits of being a full-time writer are that they confer on one a marked degree of independence and freedom, but that freedom must never be misinterpreted as irresponsibility.

I don't have to start work at nine a.m., and I don't: I usually start between six and seven in the morning. But then, though I often work a seven-day week, I don't work a fifty-two week year.

Being in a position where there is not one person, anywhere, who can tell you what to do – and that's the position I'm in – is quite splendid. But no one is wholly independent. I have a responsibility towards my publishers.

Publishing houses are not, as has been claimed, a refuge for rogues, thieves, and intellectual criminals who depend for their existence on their expertise in battening on the skills and talents of the miserably rewarded few who can do what the publishers are totally incapable of – string together a few words in a meaningful fashion. Some publishing houses are run by people who are recognisably human. Mine is notably one of those.

I feel some responsibility, though not much, to book editors. Collins New English Dictionary defines an editor as one who revises, cuts, alters, and omits in preparation for publication. I feel moderately competent to attend to the revising, cutting, etc., before it reaches the editor. But they can be of help, to some more than others.

I feel no responsibility whatsoever towards book critics. The first criticism I ever read was of my first book, H.M.S. 'Ulysses.' It got two whole pages to itself in a now defunct Scottish newspaper, with a drawing of the dust jacket wreathed in flames and the headline 'Burn this book.' I had paid the Royal Navy the greatest compliment of which I could conceive: this dolt thought it was an act of denigration.

That was the first so-called literary review I ever read: it was also the last. I'm afraid I class fiction book reviewers along with the pundits who run what it pleases them to term 'writing schools'. One must admire their courage in feeling free to advise, lecture, preach, and criticise something which they themselves are quite incapable of doing.

My greatest responsibility and debt are to those who buy my books, making it possible for me to lead the life I do. Moreover, while deriving a perfectly justifiable satisfaction in pointing out my frequent errors of fact, they never tell me how to write. I am grateful.

One great benefit arising from this freedom is the freedom to travel. I do not travel to broaden the mind or for the purposes of research. True, I have been to and written about the Arctic, the Aegean, Indonesia, Alaska, California, Yugoslavia, Holland, Brazil, and diverse other places, but I never thought of writing about these locales until I had been there: on the obverse side of the coin I have been to such disparate countries as Mexico and China, Peru and Kashmir and very much doubt whether I shall ever write about them.

About future writing I really don't know. From time to time, Mr Chapman has suggested, a trifle wistfully I always think, that some day I might get around to writing a good book. Well, it's not impossible for no doubt to the despair of all those book reviewers I never read, I wouldn't like to retire quite yet.

Seawitch

Alistair MacLean

The massive oil-rig is the hub of a great empire, the pride of its billionaire owner.

Lord Worth, predatory and ruthless, has clawed his way to great wealth. Now, he cares for only two things – *Seawitch* and his two high-spirited daughters. One man knows this:

John Cronkite, trouble-shooter for the world's top oilmen and Worth's ex-victim, is spoiling for revenge.

In one terrifying week, Worth's world explodes.

'A magnificent storyteller'   *Sunday Mirror*

'Told with all MacLean's famous gusto'   *Evening News*

'MacLean has gone back to sea – good news for anyone who likes a rip-roaring story'   *Evening Standard*

978-0-00-616474-6

Goodbye California

Alistair MacLean

'Earthquake country,'
said the Professor. 'San Francisco is geologically and seis-
mologically a city that waits to die. Los Angeles is ringed
by earthquake centres – seven massive quakes so far. We
have no idea where the next, the monster, will hit . . .'

. . . until a criminal fanatic kidnaps a nuclear scientist and
builds his own atomic bombs. If exploded on California's
fault lines they could trigger off the mightiest earthquake
of them all – killing half its population and dumping the
entire city of San Francisco into the sea.

Goodbye California . . .

'His best since *H.M.S. Ulysses*'   *Sunday Times*

'Holds the reader to the final suspenseful page'
                                                                    Sunday Telegraph

978-0-00-615360-3

Athabasca

Alistair MacLean

SABOTAGE!

THE VICTIMS
Two of the most important oil-fields in the world – one in Canada, the other in Alaska.

THE SABOTEURS
An unknown quantity – deadly and efficient. The oil flow could be interrupted in any one of thousands of places down the trans-Alaskan pipeline.

THE RESULT
Catastrophe.

One man, Jim Brady, is called in to save the life-blood of the world as unerringly, the chosen targets fall at the hands of a hidden enemy . . .

'Alistair MacLean is a magnificent storyteller'
Sunday Mirror

'The most successful British novelist of his time'
Jack Higgins

978-0-00-616266-7

River of Death

Alistair MacLean

Hamilton knows the way to the ruins deep in the Brazilian jungle – and the secret they hold.

The millionaire who calls himself Smith seeks the lost city to avenge a wrong from his hidden past.

Their journey down the River of Death is an epic of violence and danger. But the secret that awaits them in the lost city is more dangerous still – as a legacy of theft, treachery and murder stretching back to war-torn Europe comes to a deadly climax beneath the ancient walls.

'A magnificent storyteller'   *Sunday Mirror*

'The most successful British novelist of his time'
                                                Jack Higgins

978-0-00-616496-8